WHAT OTHERS SAY

Unwrapping Your Passion

Karen's courageous return to her passion decades after abandoning it—and the joy she continues to reap from having done so—is a story that inspires me greatly. We would all do well to be like Karen in this way. I'm glad she wrote this book so that her story and the other stories she shares can inspire you to max out your joy.

Shaun Proulx

speaker, author, columnist, radio/TV personality
sharing a #ThoughtRevolution about personal limits

When you follow Karen Putz's formula for Unwrapping Your Passions, the gift you'll find inside right next to your passions will be deep, true, and lasting happiness.

Marci Shimoff

NY Times Bestselling Author of
Happy for No Reason

Life is too short to live it any other way than a breath-taking adventure. Here's a book that will help you do that.

Randy Gage

author of *Risky Is the New Safe*

If you want to shift from being awake to being ALIVE, this is the book you must pick up and devour from cover to cover. Karen is the personification of doing whatever it takes to leverage the gifts one has been given and sharing one's unique ability with strategic abandon. You were born to do something amazing. Unwrapping Your Passion teaches you how to identify what it is.

Steve Olsher

New York Times bestselling author of *What Is Your WHAT? Discover The ONE Amazing Thing You Were Born to Do*

Some fear that following our passion is a selfish pursuit, in opposition to serving others well. I believe digging deeply to find our own unique passion opens us up to our greatest opportunity for making the world a better place, not through trying but by being authentic. Unwrapping Your Passion is the guide you've been waiting for. Now discover your passion and experience the joy Karen can't hide—the thing that makes others want what she has.

Dan Miller

NY Times bestselling author and coach (48Days.com)

I was fortunate to unwrap my passion for swimming at a young age and that very passion propelled me through the Olympics multiple times in a 24 year span. Unwrapping Your Passion produces a fresh look at what it takes to live a passionate, full life.

Dara Torres

Age is Just a Number, Achieve Your Dreams at Any Stage in Your Life

We all have a responsibility. A responsibility to ourselves, our family, and to those closest to us, to live a life of fun, excitement, and fullness. Unfortunately, the demands and stressors of work and life can cause us to lose track of what we once knew; leaving us listless, empty, and filled with unanswered questions.

In Karen Putz's groundbreaking book, Unwrapping your Passion, she brilliantly helps us understand what passion is, what it is for us, and why we can no longer afford to ignore it.

Your passion is a gift from God. What you choose to do with it, is your gift back.

Joel Boggess
author, podcaster, speaker, The ReLaunch Show

The time is now for you to embrace your true calling and follow your passion and purpose. Karen will inspire you to dig deeper to find your authentic self. Her powerful questions and engaging stories will bring you an understanding of your own passions and how to pursue them. Unwrapping Your Passion is a must read for anyone who is ready for a rewarding life doing what they are uniquely designed to do.

Jackie Wellwood
author of *Lead With Your Integrity: Choosing to Follow Your Moral Code Regardless of Circumstances*

Karen's enthusiastic and passionate nature can't help but draw you into this book. She is adamant that everyone is capable of more than they realize and age or disability is not a deterrant to achieving AWE moments. Playing it safe doesn't allow for for a life of passion and AWE and Karen challenges the reader to put aside fear and the mundane. From the beginning I was drawn into the stories, examples and challenges Karen puts forth in this book. You will be too!

Joanne F. Miller

author of *Creating a Haven of Peace*

It's all too easy to get caught up in daily routines and settle into a mediocre rhythm in life. Unwrapping Your Passion will challenge you to dig deep into what you've always wanted to do to create a life you truly love. Karen Putz reminded me of how important it is to keep writing (which is my passion), despite all the other forces that conspire against us.

Lee Woodruff

author of *Perfectly Imperfect: A Life in Progress*

Unwrapping Your Passion

UNWRAPPING YOUR PASSION

Creating the Life You Truly Want

KAREN PUTZ

NEW YORK

NASHVILLE • MELBOURNE • VANCOUVER

Unwrapping Your Passion

Creating the Life You Truly Want

Published in New York, New York, by Morgan James Publishing. Morgan James is a trademark of Morgan James, LLC. www.MorganJamesPublishing.com

The Morgan James Speakers Group can bring authors to your live event. For more information or to book an event visit The Morgan James Speakers Group at www.TheMorganJamesSpeakersGroup.com.

Address all author inquiries to:

Karen Putz
karen@agelesspassions.com
www.UnwrappingYourPassion.com

Every attempt has been made to source properly all quotes. For additional copies visit:
www.UnwrappingYourPassion.com

Cover Design by:
Chris Treccani
www.3dogdesign.net

Interior Design by:
Chris Treccani
www.3dogdesign.net

ISBN 9781683504757 paperback
ISBN 9781683504764 eBook
ISBN 9781683504771 hardcover
Library of Congress Control Number: 2017902635

Editor:
Tyler Tichelaar
Superior Book Productions

In an effort to support local communities, raise awareness and funds, Morgan James Publishing donates a percentage of all book sales for the life of each book to Habitat for Humanity Peninsula and Greater Williamsburg.

Get involved today! Visit
www.MorganJamesBuilds.com

FOR PATTI PHADKE,

my wonderful friend who taught me

that passion is not only the fire in the belly,

but also the quiet nudging from the heart.

PASSION

It begins with a tiny spark, a soft
nudge, or
A gentle awakening.
It becomes a racing heart, a burning
desire,
And fuel for life.
Passion is your joy.
It is the essence of who you are—
And within the many layers of your
soul
Lies the gift of passion.
Unwrap yours.

CONTENTS

FOREWORD

By Janet Attwood and Debra Poneman

We met the amazing Karen Putz a few months apart when she attended our respective seminars. We both agreed that her joy, enthusiasm, and brilliance were utterly contagious and she was a standout in the crowd. We also agreed on one other thing: *When we grew up, we wanted to be just like her.*

Yes, we were the ones with the impressive credentials and the best-selling books. We were the ones who traveled the globe sharing our programs in order to make the world a better place one speech, one seminar, one TV interview, one summit, one life at a time.

But Karen—beautiful, radiant, Karen…smiley, friendly, buoyant, loving, giving, insightful, soulful, live-life-full-out Karen soon became not only our dear friend but one of our greatest inspirations.

Whenever one of us refers to Karen for any reason, the other spontaneously adds some rendition of "Is there anyone with a more beautiful heart?" or "How amazing is that woman?" or "Could you love her any more?" and more often than not, we move on to reflect upon *who we would be if we were out water skiing with friends, laughing and talking one minute and deaf the next.*

Would we have the courage to use the techniques we teach about going with the flow and loving what is, or would we retreat to a place of "This isn't fair" and "Why me"?

Would we stop trusting in the perfection of the universe and stop believing that the Universe has our backs? *Or would we grieve and cry our eyes out for a few weeks and then say, "Okay, now it's time to rock this being deaf thing"?*

How can you not want to learn from a woman who not only rocks "the deaf journey," but, instead of wallowing in any self-pity, goes on also to rock the writing journey and the barefoot skiing journey and the mom journey and the public speaking journey and now the journey of sharing with the world how to *unwrap your passions.*

And we want to make it clear that this isn't a book by a deaf lady or even a deaf barefoot skiing mom. This is a book by a powerful woman who wants no preferential treatment for being differently abled. This is a book that will inspire you to come alive, to celebrate your uniqueness, to stop letting life happen and start making life happen, to understand fear for the imposter it really is—and to dust off your passions and live the life you were put on earth to live no matter what kind of "abled" you are.

If living a passionate life now—not next week or in five years—is the message, Karen Putz is living proof that that is possible for us all. She not only walks her talk, but as one writer described her: "Karen Putz is someone who literally walks on water." We couldn't agree more. Once you read this book, hear her story, and embrace her guidance, we're sure you'll agree as well.

Debra Poneman, bestselling author and founder of *Yes to Success, Inc.* and co-founder of Your Year of Miracles, LLC

Janet Attwood, *NY Times* bestselling author and co-founder of The Passion Test

INTRODUCTION

"Everyone is gifted—but some people never open their package."
~ **Author Unknown**

A re you hitting the snooze button twenty times in a row on the days you have to get up for work? Have you settled into a "ho-hum" routine? Do you wait in eager anticipation for the weekends so you can finally enjoy life?

Does this describe you?

If so, you're not alone. A 2013 Gallup Poll on the State of the American Workplace showed that 70 percent of 150,000 people surveyed were "disengaged from their work."

That's a nice way of saying people hate their jobs.

Maybe hate is too strong of a word, but think about this: only 30 percent of those polled actually *enjoy* their work. We don't even know whether those people are passionately in love with what they do—just that they enjoy their jobs and their bosses.

A couple of years ago, that was me. I worked in a company that I liked with a boss whom I enjoyed. I just wasn't passionately in love with what I was doing. Some months I did my job well—I was the third employee to earn the highest monthly bonus for sales. Yet something was missing:

Passion.

So I set out on a journey to learn from people who were madly, passionately in love with life and what they do. This book is a result of that journey. In each chapter, you will find stories of people who unwrapped their passions and created lives of joy and fulfillment.

What I hope you get from this book is the ability to unwrap all the layers of you and get to the nitty-gritty of "This is who I am. This is what I was born for. This is what I love to do."

It's a common question: "How do I find my passion?"

This is a question I've been exploring with others ever since I unwrapped a long-buried passion of mine at the age of forty-four. I will dive into my story about this passion in the next chapter. Meanwhile, let me share another passion of mine.

I love to write. I unwrapped the gift of writing when I was nine. One summer day, I was quite bored at home, so I decided to write a story. It was a fiction masterpiece that was all of four paragraphs long. As I sat at my father's typewriter (Typewriter? I know some of you are scurrying to Google right now) and pounded the keys, I discovered I really enjoyed the process of putting my thoughts in written form.

Over the years, I dabbled in that passion, writing for the school newspaper, a writing company, a non-profit organization, and various newsletters. Then I became a blogger and wrote for online sites like Disaboom, Parenting Squad, Ricky Martin's Piccolo Universe, and Chicago Moms. For a short time, I wrote for the TribLocal section of the *Chicago Tribune*. It was fun to see my columns in print each week.

I could interview people for hours and then turn around and tell their stories using the written word. In the early years of unwrapping this gift, people would call me nosy. I always wanted to know what made them tick. I wanted to know what they were feeling. I wanted to know their dreams, their joys, and...their passions. I used to ask questions until people told me I was getting in too deep—and then I backed off.

One evening, I was taking a long soak in the bathtub and reading through underlined passages from the book *Aspire* by Kevin Hall. I had just finished reading *The Passion Test* by Janet and Chris Attwood. I sat there for a long time, pondering the different passions in my life.

As I was meditating upon the question of my next book, suddenly a book appeared before my eyes:

Unwrapping Your Passion.

On the cover, I could see a large, fluffy bow. The entire book looked like a gift. I thought about how I had unwrapped my own passions, and I wanted to share my newfound knowledge with others. I was so excited that I jumped out of the bathtub, threw on a towel, and ran downstairs to see whether the domain, www.UnwrappingYourPassion.com, was available. It was. Right then and there, I purchased the domain.

But the time wasn't right for me to begin writing. I had some passionate living of my own to do first. There was no way I could write a book about passion without experiencing it firsthand and learning from others.

In the beginning, I was stumped. Where to start? How would I find people who were truly living passionate lives? I reached out to Kevin Hall and asked him those very questions. Here is what he told me:

"Dive in with all your heart, follow your bliss, and people will appear to help you with what you want most."

So following Kevin's advice, I dove into my passions. I barefoot water skied every chance I could get. I wrote and I wrote—blog posts, magazine articles, newspaper articles, and books. I became a Certified

Passion Test Facilitator and used that tool to help other people discover their top five passions. I became a speaker and traveled internationally to Canada, Austria, and Russia.

Sure enough, just as Kevin predicted, people appeared in my life left and right. Time and time again, Kevin's wisdom proved to be true. At every turn, I crossed paths with some amazing people. The same thing will happen to you on your own journey of passion—the key is to be open to the possibilities and opportunities that show up along the journey.

During a flight home after a trip, I started writing down the names of people I wanted to interview for this book. After I wrote a couple of names down, I looked at the dismally short list and wondered how I was going to meet even more passionate people to fill this book. At that point, I was still at the beginning of my own journey of unwrapping my passions and most of my friends were living the same typical "Midwest suburban" lifestyle as I was.

My eyes drifted to the guy sitting next to me, who was reading a book. I strained to see the title. The very first word that popped out at me was:

Passion.

My heart started to beat faster. The title of the book was *How to Turn Your Passion into Cash.*

Okay, that was a sign if I ever saw one! I turned to the guy, pointed to the book, and asked him, "So what's your passion?"

As it turned out, Pete Gluzsek was passionate about fishing. He loved it so much that he dove into it full-time and made his passion his profession. He left a nice, solid job with benefits to become a professional bass fisherman. Every chance he gets, Pete is out on the water reeling in bass. If you open a fishing magazine, chances are you'll find a picture of Pete holding his latest catch. You may even see him on ESPN during a fishing tournament. You'll find more of Pete's story later in the book.

For many of us, the typical way of life is the safe, complacent one. We've been taught to go to school, do well, get a job, and then live for retirement. If you play your cards right, you'll have enough money and good health so you can finally play and enjoy life in retirement. Only then can you release your passion and pursue the things you love to do.

In reality, that's a risky gamble. At any given moment, life can change on a dime.

When I rediscovered a long-buried passion of my youthful days, I found joy again. The joy was evident in the pictures I posted on Facebook. One day, a coworker said to me, "I want what you have. That."

"What is 'that'?" I asked.

"That passion on your face. How do I get that?"

So right then and there, I gave her the Passion Test, a tool developed by Janet and Chris Attwood, which identifies and prioritizes your top five passions. To her complete surprise, the number one thing on her list was to ride a tandem bike with her husband. The couple had become so entrenched in reacting to life's routine that they kept putting off the one thing that brought them pleasure.

A month later, I received a happy email from her. She and her husband brought their bike out and rode together.

In the snow. In the middle of January, mind you. On a mountain, no less.

Passion doesn't have to wait.

So what if, instead of the typical life, you incorporated passion into your everyday life? How much different would life be if you aligned your skills, gifts, and heart into something you really love to do?

You might be afraid of what you're going to find if you peel back those layers toward passion. You might be holding back because the dream is too big, too scary. And deep down, you might be scared of this thought: What if I fail?

But what if you succeed? What if you discover a life aligned with your passions so you look forward to each day with relish? How much different would life be if you could wake up knowing you could dive deep into something you truly love to do, something you're gifted with, something that fires up your soul?

That early lesson from Kevin Hall was a powerful one—he taught me to focus on bliss. The Yes to Success workshop by Debra Poneman opened my eyes to a whole new world. The Passion Test by Janet Attwood changed my life. Dan Miller's books and workshop set me on the path to writing books. Throughout this book, I will share even more lessons with you from all the awesome, passionate people I met on this journey. They all had their own individual journeys to unwrapping their passions.

Now let's unwrap yours.

CHAPTER 1

Unwrapping My Passion

*"Each of us is born with a unique
life purpose."*
~ Jack Canfield

I remember my forty-fourth birthday pretty well. I sat in a pontoon on Christie Lake, watching a water skier zip by. I wasn't in a celebratory mood—if anything, I just felt incredibly *blah*. My days had become pretty routine. I had a sales job I actually liked at the time. I was traveling, meeting new people, and learning about sales. Life wasn't bad at all—it was just *ho-hum*.

Another boat went by. I reflected on my life. I thought back to some happy times and remembered moments of joy: getting married, buying a tiny house, building a bigger house, having kids, and moving into yet another bigger house.

My mind drifted way back—all the way back to my teen years. I remembered an unbridled feeling of joy. It was a joy unlike anything else I've ever experienced.

Barefoot water skiing.

You see, that sport was a crazy passion of mine. I absolutely loved the feeling of skimming on the water behind a boat with nothing between me and the water. It was a skill that no other female on the lake could match. This meant I skied with guys—and that was more than fine by me! Barefoot water skiing was the great equalizer for me. For most of my life, I had struggled to fit in and be like everyone else. I started losing my hearing in elementary school and received my first hearing aid at age nine. I hated being different. I hated being hard of hearing. I hid my hearing aid every chance I could and never wore it in the summer.

One August day, my life took a very different turn. I took a couple of barefooting runs around the lake, and during one run, I decided to cross the wake. I had done it once before with success and wanted to try it again. I told my friend to go a little faster than usual so the wake would be flatter and easier to cross. My foot caught in the wake and I cart-wheeled into the water. In an instant, I went from hard of hearing to deaf.

Oh yeah, life took a very different turn.

When I climbed into the boat, I could no longer hear my friends' voices. Their lips moved, but no sound came out. Hmmm, maybe my ears were just temporarily filled with water.

I kept hoping I would get my hearing back, but as it turned out, being deaf was here to stay. On the morning I was getting ready to leave for college, I broke down crying at the door.

"What's wrong?" my mom asked.

"I can't hear anything anymore."

My mom started crying too. "You don't have to go to college," she said. "You can stay home and get a job."

But staying home was not what I wanted. I had already spent a year at a local community college and I was lonely. I wanted more—but I didn't know what I wanted. Living away from home seemed to be the answer.

When I arrived on campus, I discovered I was placed in a dorm with other deaf and hard of hearing students. I was not happy. I marched down to the information desk and demanded to be moved to a "normal" dorm.

"Give it a try," my mom urged. "You might make some new friends here." (Moms are always right—I met my husband!)

I didn't adjust very well at first. I spent my days struggling in the classroom trying to lipread my professors. I spent my nights crying. I was uncomfortable around people whose hands were flying with American Sign Language.

For the first few months following my sudden plunge into deafness, I was frustrated and bitter. I hid my feelings because it was very difficult to talk about it.

One morning, I had an epiphany: I could continue to struggle, mourn, and grieve, or I could change my attitude and become the best possible deaf person I could be. I made my decision. I was going to embrace the Deaf Journey. I slapped my hearing aid on my right ear, put my hair up in a ponytail, and walked out the door. I had never shown my hearing aid in public before. That decision changed everything for me.

This reminds me of the metamorphosis that a caterpillar goes through to become a butterfly. The caterpillar thinks his life is over. In reality, the end of being a caterpillar is simply the beginning of a beautiful life as a butterfly.

(And what do you know, butterflies don't have ears—they're deaf!)

Because of that metamorphosis, I ended up meeting some really awesome deaf and hard of hearing people, and I learned American Sign Language. I slowly abandoned barefoot water skiing and stopped when I was twenty-four. The last time I put my feet on the water was just once after my oldest child was born. I was twenty-seven. From then on, my feet never touched the water again until I tried barefooting the day before my forty-fourth birthday. I was over 200 pounds and very out of shape.

So there I was on my birthday, thinking back to the old passion I used to have for the sport. I had dreams back then. I wanted to compete in barefoot tournaments. I contemplated colleges with water-ski programs. I imagined myself barefooting in water skiing shows.

None of that ever happened.

While I was sitting in the boat, tears began to fall. I was filled with regret. *Why didn't I pursue the sport while I was younger? Why didn't I appreciate barefooting when I could still do it?* Forty-four seemed so ancient for such an extreme sport. Suddenly, a thought hit me—I probably would never barefoot water ski again. I was too old, too overweight, and too out of shape, I thought. The tears just fell harder.

I went back home to my ho-hum life.

A *TODAY Show* Segment Changed My Life

As I was cleaning out my email box several weeks later, I noticed an email from my husband with a *TODAY Show* link. The segment featured Judy Myers, a sixty-six-year-old competitive barefoot water skier with a shock of blond-white hair. I clicked "play" and watched the "Old Lady" glide on the water.

Sixty-six years old.

What's more, she took up the extreme sport at the age of...fifty-three.

Wait a minute—I was only forty-four.

As I replayed the video, tears began to fall, this time with hope. If this sixty-six-year-old woman could enjoy the sport, surely I could get back on the water again.

When I connected with Judy through Facebook, she invited me down to Florida to take a lesson at a barefoot water ski school. I booked the trip during the kids' spring break.

I was nervous when I arrived at the World Barefoot Center in Winter Haven, Florida. Judy was all smiles and she led me to the dock. Just getting into a wetsuit was a workout. I was very much out-of-shape and carrying a lot of extra pounds. I got into the boat with four other skiers who were very experienced.

Keith St. Onge, the two-time World Barefoot Champion and our instructor, invited me to go first. I shook my head. I just wasn't ready. My nerves were too jangled.

The other skiers took turns doing tumble turns on their backs, lifting one foot in the air, and skiing backwards on their feet. I was amazed. I had never seen anyone barefoot water ski backwards, much less a woman over sixty who skied with ease.

Then it was my turn.

I got in the water, gripped the boom, and the boat took off. The minute I put my feet in the water, time stood still. I was a teenager again. The smile on my face would have lit up a galaxy.

Fast forward to today—if you had told me as a teen that at the age of fifty I would be able to barefoot water ski backwards on one foot with my hands in the air, I would have laughed so hard I would have ended up with a hernia.

Since that pivotal moment, life was never the same. I was hungry for more, and I wanted to share what I had learned with others.

The biggest lesson on this journey to passion is this: We are capable of far more than we realize—and we can choose a passionate life at any age.

> *"There is no end. There is no beginning. There is only the passion of life."*
> ~ Federico Fellini

If you're skeptical about this whole passion thing, I urge you to keep an open mind and to be willing to soak in new knowledge. Living a life that is rich with passion, joy, and fulfillment—I promise you, it's worth it.

CHAPTER 2

Defining Passion

"For the most part we all need to honor ourselves more, appreciate our individual strengths, and seek and approach life with maximum passion."
~ Werner Berger, who climbed Mt. Everest at age sixty-nine

Remember what it was like when you were a kid? You were wrapped up deep in yourself. Finding joy was usually a simple thing. The thing you liked to do, you did over and over again. You laughed when you were happy. You cried when you were sad. But what happens to us as we grow up? It seems like we take on lives of mediocrity and comfort. We stuff down how we really feel.

What if you changed that scenario? What if you learned to unwrap your gifts and discover just what it is that lights your soul on fire? What if, every day, you could wake up excited and jump out of bed looking forward to the creation of each day?

You absolutely can.

Brendon Burchard calls this passionate, energized approach the "Charged Life." At the end of our life, we will ask ourselves three questions, "Did I live? Did I love? Did I matter?"

What if we asked ourselves those questions *now*, and we changed the course of our lives so the answers are to our satisfaction?

You absolutely can. The key is to utilize passion as a guide.

What Is This Thing Called Passion?

Passion.

Every time I see that word, I get all fired up. Try saying it in a flat, monotone voice. I bet you can't. /PaSHen/, baby! You can't help but put a little "oomph" into it. That's exactly what passion does in your life—it puts a little "oomph" into everything you do. One way to look at it is to see passion as the soul on fire. The deep burning within to do the thing you were born to do.

But…passion is also the quiet nudge within that tells you when you're feeling blissful and content.

"Passion is something you just can't wait to do. It's something that wakes you up early and keeps you up late at night. When you are doing what you're passionate about, you lose track of time because you're enjoying it so much."
~ **Joel Boggess**, *The ReLaunch Show*

Perhaps the best definition of passion I've ever come across is from Jackie St. Onge, mother of two-time World Barefoot Champion, Keith St. Onge:

"Passion is your joy. It is the essence of who you are. You have to unwrap it to find it. The mind, body, and soul become one when you find it. Passion comes naturally to a person. It's like running water; turn on the tap and it flows."

It seems pretty simple, doesn't it? Discover that which "flows" within you and you've unwrapped your passion.

So why do we make it so complicated?

The most passionate people I crossed paths with often couldn't explain the "why" of what they do—but they could explain the joy—the fired up feeling, the bliss, the grip of their passion.

Passion is energy. It's a feeling, an emotion, a desire, and a purpose all rolled into one.

A friend once told me she felt the word "passion" was way overused. "You need to change the title of your book," she advised. "It's just too cliché."

Are you kidding me?

When I look around and see the many souls who are trudging through life with a dull look in their eyes, I realize we need an awakening—a *passionate* awakening to all the possibilities of life that occur when you're engaged in something you're truly passionate about. We need to infuse passion into our daily lives. Imagine how much happier our world would be if everyone were passionately engaged in something he or she truly enjoys. Imagine the kind of energy that would radiate forth!

I've also been told I use the word "passion" way too much when I speak.

So you've been warned…this is a book about passion. I'm going to talk about it in depth, and I'm going to use the word "passion" a lot.

Joel Boggess, a life coach who is a great friend of mine, often finds that the word "passion" can be difficult for some people; they shut down when they try to explore their passions and their purposes.

"Passion is a confusing term sometimes," Joel told me. "People don't know whether they've felt passion during their lives so I use the word 'excitement' instead. It's a word people can wrap themselves around, and it helps me initiate a conversation to analyze their passions in a deeper way."

As soon as we start defining ourselves, we begin to set up boxes around who we are and what we do.

If you feel a desire inside to do something bigger than what you're doing now, chances are you have a passion waiting to be unwrapped. That desire, that longing, is a prompting to discover more about yourself and what matters to you in life.

Passion. Excitement. Joy. We're going to increase all of those terms in your life. You just have to be willing to be open to them.

Peel Back the Layers, Baby!

Another way to recognize passion is to be aware of what you desire. So let's try a little writing exercise here. What do you wish for?

I wish I...

_____

_____

_____

_____

How would you finish that sentence? Go ahead and write down what you're thinking before you read any further.

Now I want you to shift a bit and think of an onion. Passion has layers—just like an onion. For some of us, the outer layers are easy to get to. We find passion quickly—or passion finds us. For others, we have to peel back the layers to reach that place of clarity. Some of us have to go through layers and layers of life experiences to reach that place of alignment.

Now, an onion is a living thing with a pretty long shelf life, but if you neglect it long enough, eventually, your place is going to stink.

So that's how it is with this whole passion business. Ignore the passion inside of you, and your life is going to stink. Ignore your desires, your talents, your longings—and, eventually, they're going to catch up with you in the energy of regret.

The Surprising Meaning of Passion

Now let's go a little deeper. The feelings of joy and excitement are momentous—meaning that we can't sustain them every minute of our lives. This is why passion is so much more than just feelings. Passion is energy, but energy with a purpose.

It might totally surprise you to learn that the root meaning of passion is "to be willing to suffer for what you love." Yes, that's right. *To suffer willingly.* Kevin Hall explains this in his book, *Aspire: The Power of Words*. In his quest to understand the meaning behind eleven powerful words, Kevin turned to the Master of Words, Arthur Watkins, who taught him the meaning of words and how they can have a profound influence on our lives.

"At the essence," Arthur explains, "passion is sacred suffering."

"And suffering isn't necessarily a bad thing," Kevin writes in *Aspire*. "It can and should be a good thing. It's noble. It's sacred. It's life defining."

Kevin discovered a love for speaking at an early age. Whenever he stood in front of the class to speak or give a report, he enjoyed the attention he received. In contrast, he struggled with biology and science classes. Clearly, a future in those areas was not lined up with his skills, nor his passion.

Kevin's gift with words enabled him to create a stellar career in sales, first with Yellow Pages (he became the top advertising salesman within three months after being hired) and with Franklin Covey (VP of Sales and Training in a half-billion dollar company). During his time at Franklin Covey, Kevin spent two days at the Johnson O'Connor Research Facility, being tested in all different areas to determine his skills and unique gifts.

To his great surprise, the tests showed Kevin's strongest strength was in the area of ideaphoria. He could take a single word and come up with pages and pages of ideas centered around that word. Kevin went on to create work that focused on connecting words, ideas, and people.

"I believe it's within our capacity and our potential if it fits with our God-given gifts; there's nothing we can't do and it's up to us to do it," Kevin says. "When you go after something with your whole heart and soul, the universe conspires to make it happen. When you make a decision, it becomes an action."

People who are stuck in a routine or those who cease to dream are functioning from a place of fear, Kevin explains. Fear feeds the idea that we are not enough. "It creates a 'scarcity mentality'," Kevin says. "If you believe you are not enough, you won't be able to achieve your dreams."

For many years, I believed I was not enough. I was just a wife. Just a mom. Just an ordinary person. Those crazy people out there living their dreams—well, they had some kind of special formula that just didn't apply to me.

In the last several years, I've been studying everything I can on the topic of passion. I've come to understand this:

We are beautifully unique for a reason. There's no one else in the whole wide world just like you. We each have the capability within us to create and live passion-filled lives. In the upcoming chapters, we're going to dive deeper into this process.

> "When you expire, you cease to breathe;
> when you inspire, you breathe life. When
> we quit breathing and quit dreaming,
> we expire, and sometimes people do that
> when they are still alive."
> ~ Kevin Hall

Jessica Semaan: Your Soul Coming Alive

During one of my many web searches on the topic of passion, Jessica Semaan's name came up. Jessica left a lucrative job at AirBnB to create The Passion Co., a business designed to help others discover their passions. Her website features stories of people who are living passionate lives. In an interview I conducted with Jessica, she enthusiastically shared her thoughts and views on the topic.

"The world really needs you to find what you want to do and do it," Jessica told me. "There is a lot of suffering and misery and hatred in the world and you have the power in your own way to change that by taking a stance and saying 'I'm gonna live a life that I love. I'm gonna live a life that's meaningful, that's gonna make a difference.' So the world needs you to follow your passion."

During her studies at Stanford Business School, Jessica Semaan was depressed, but she didn't really know it. She just felt empty. Sad. Life didn't matter anymore—she no longer wanted to be here.

The dark feelings were a surprising turn for Jessica. She had come to Stanford from Lebanon, and she had thought the move would pave the way for a happy life.

During a counseling session, a therapist asked her, "Do you love yourself?"

The question startled Jessica. *Love? Herself?*

"I was confused, I wasn't sure what the therapist was talking about," Jessica explains. "Then I realized I didn't know who I was to love myself. When I meet a new person, I get to know them and love them. I didn't know myself."

That question led Jessica on a journey to discover and love herself. She began facing long-buried fears and began to reconnect with her childhood. During the process of peeling back the layers, Jessica came to realize that she had buried many of her passions, especially dancing and writing. Her creative side had not been touched in years.

Her first writing project was to interview people about passion. One by one, as the stories unfolded, Jessica found herself with a whole new energy.

"My life became exciting. I woke up feeling ready to take over the day," she said.

She ended up interviewing 100 people and exploring how passion appears and evolves. Jessica was doing all of this on the side, finding time around her job at Airbnb. She was also fortunate to have a wonderful mentor at Airbnb, Chip Conley, whose passion is to help others find and create lives of meaning.

When Jessica was asked to speak at a work-related event, she discovered another layer of passion when she stepped on the stage.

She came alive.

That's exactly how Jessica explains passion: it is your soul coming alive.

And like Kevin Hall, Jessica also finds that passion is rooted in suffering.

"Passion—I think of it as suffering; that's what the word means in Latin," she said. "I think of raw and human energy. Passion is our gift to the world. It is when we are being our most honest, inside child without fear. Passion is more than one thing—it is life."

"So why, then, are so many of us numb to it?" I asked her.

"I think it's because of our society structure," she said. "Since you're a kid, you're told what is right and what is wrong. Do this. Don't do that. You can't develop the ability to go with feelings—of feeling fear or living with excitement or daring. So I think we become programmed not to feel our feelings. We don't have that capacity to feel when we are older until something traumatic or something bad happens to wake us up. We have to learn to love ourselves and to dare to dream."

Can you relate to what Jessica shared? This leads me to ask: What happens to us as adults that drives us to that place where we've learned to trudge through daily life? Why do we lose that childlike ability to explore life and honor that place inside of us that harbors our joy?

There's a big difference between willingly suffering for something that is driven by passion versus suffering for something that is sucking the very life out of your soul. If you're driven by passion, you will feel aligned with your path and will have the energy to tackle the obstacles in your way.

"Man is so made that when anything fires his soul, impossibilities vanish."
~ Jean de la Fontaine

Welcome Suffering

Now that you know the surprising meaning behind passion, which is the willingness to suffer, you'll probably look at passion in a whole different light when you're deep in the middle of something you truly enjoy. You will put in the extra effort to go above and beyond when you're on a passionate path.

Jay Heinrichs, editor of *Southwest Magazine*, described his suffering in intense detail when he set up a personal challenge to sprint up a mountain for his fifty-eighth birthday. In an article entitled "The Mountain of Youth," Jay describes how he endured 330 injections of dextrose into his ailing hip in an attempt to walk normally again. To prepare himself for the fifty-eight-minute climb, Jay woke up at 4 a.m. to train an average of three hours a day. He gave up drinking, Netflix, and his social life. All for a personal quest that meant nothing to everyone else, but meant everything to him.

On the day of his birthday, Jay put himself to the test. With every asthma-induced breath, he willed himself up the path and over rocks. The higher he climbed, the happier he became. Whether he would meet his goal or not, he came to realize the effort, the conquest, and the journey were the real goals after all.

To his great surprise, he reached the end with a time of 54:53—far better than he had ever dreamt.

Suffering, Jay learned, can lead to incredible victory.

"I learned about suffering from the legendary distance runner Steve Prefontaine, who famously said that while he wasn't the best at running, he could suffer more than anyone," Jay writes. "He bore more, pushing his imperfect body to one record after another. To 'suffer' means to allow, even welcome. It moves beyond pain, because this welcoming of the overwhelming isn't pain at all. It's life with all the stops open."

Life with all the stops open. Can you imagine living that way? Can you imagine the joy that comes with that formula for life?

But there's more.

Jay believes we need more "awe experiences" in our lives. Those are the experiences where we step back and look at ourselves with complete awe—experiences that stretch us above and beyond what we believe is possible for ourselves. It's the feeling of "Holy moly, *that's* freakin' awesome."

"I believe that you feel greater awe when you've overcome obstacles to confront something vast and scary," Jay writes.

I've had many of what I'm calling "Awe Moments" since getting back on the water. If you remember from my story, I was overweight and very out-of-shape when I took up barefoot water skiing again. Water skiing on bare feet is definitely not an easy sport, even for the most athletically fit. I once spent ten days on the water training with World Champions and pushing myself in ways that I couldn't even imagine as a teenager, much less as a woman approaching fifty. I was sore. Every part of my body creaked and groaned each morning when I climbed out of bed. There were some days I felt as if I made little or no progress. On the very last day, one of my coaches set me up to do what's called a "Back Toe Hold." It requires barefoot water skiing backwards on one foot, with the other foot holding a strap on the handle, and both hands in the air. As you can imagine, it's a scary thing to do. One wrong move and you find yourself doing the splits backward at 39 mph.

I could have played it safe and declined to try. But here's the thing with playing it safe: You never set yourself up for experiencing Awe Moments.

So I went for it. I let go of the handle and found myself gliding along backwards on one foot with my hands in the air.

Holy moly, that's freakin awesome!

It was an Awe Moment I'll always remember.

And the awe that comes with accomplishing something you've worked for, sweated for, and passionately aimed for?

Priceless.

When was the last time you had an Awe Moment in your life? What is an Awe Moment you'd like to go for?

_____

_____

_____

_____

Suffering for What You Love vs. Suffering for the Wrong Thing

There's a big difference between suffering for something you love or truly want, versus suffering for something that has little or no meaning to you.

Suffering for the wrong thing is like running a marathon in the wrong direction—the whole time you're not sure where the finish line is (or it's so far away that you've lost hope) and it takes tremendous energy even to keep going. Suffering for the wrong thing is like climbing up a very long ladder, only to discover you've set it against the wrong wall. You get the idea.

I taught American Sign Language for many years at a local college. For the first several years, I loved it. After a while, I began to dread the beginning of each semester—yet I loved speaking to the class and making people laugh. Finally, I came to a point where I didn't want to continue. I realized I wanted to speak to people and entertain them, not teach course work. After fifteen years of teaching, I left. Several times in the years since, I've been offered teaching positions, but I've declined them. My heart was no longer in the work, so it was not my path.

When you encounter the "I don't want to do this" feeling, you're being moved toward something more. This is *growth*.

> *"Being passionate about something means you're willing to be vested in it through thick and thin."*
> ~ Karen Putz

At a *One Day to Greatness* workshop in Chicago, Jack Canfield talked about his own revelation of discovering he no longer had the passion to continue to produce Chicken Soup for the Soul books. He was not having fun. He was no longer looking forward to each new project. He was totally bored, he told the audience. He and Mark Victor Hansen sold their company and moved on to more exciting projects that were lined up with their passion and purpose.

When the purpose, the meaning, and the why of what you're doing is lined up with something your heart truly beats for, then you'll endure the suffering. Passion will pull you through it.

In his book, *Man's Search for Meaning*, Holocaust survivor Viktor Frankl taught us, man can endure any "how" if the "why" is strong enough. "When we are no longer able to change a situation, we are challenged to change ourselves," he wrote. Even in the most horrific conditions, Viktor was able to choose his attitude, his thoughts, and his actions in the prison.

A sense of purpose and meaning leads to fulfillment in life. Pause here and ask yourself the "why" of what you do, or what you want to do. What's driving you? What's the why behind it?

_____

_____

_____

_____

_____

_____

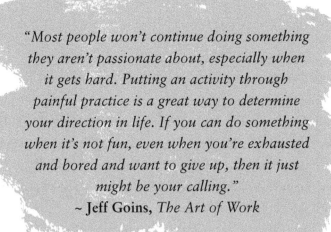

"Most people won't continue doing something they aren't passionate about, especially when it gets hard. Putting an activity through painful practice is a great way to determine your direction in life. If you can do something when it's not fun, even when you're exhausted and bored and want to give up, then it just might be your calling."
~ **Jeff Goins**, *The Art of Work*

The Diversity of Passion

I used to think I was really weird because my life wasn't typical after I graduated from college. I worked many different jobs while my kids were growing up. Retail, printing, substitute teaching, early intervention, writing, non-profit, sales, management, and speaking. I always felt (and still do) as if I have multiple interests and I'm passionate about many of them. Jeff Goins, author of *The Art of Work*, calls this multi-talent/multi-interest the "Portfolio Life." A portfolio life isn't just about what you do, it's about who you are, Jeff explains on his blog, goinswriter.com. As a dreamer who constantly tries new things and re-invents new paths—this was my fit.

Emilie Wapnick, in her TEDx talk, "Why Some of Us Don't Have One True Calling," specifically addresses the idea of one having too many passions; she calls such persons "multipotentialites," people who have a range of interests and jobs over one lifetime. Dorie Clark, a marketing strategy consultant, speaker, author, and comedian, has another name for those who are passionately immersed in many things: "Renaissance people."

For many years, I struggled with my constant desire to jump into new things, new experiences, and new directions. I couldn't understand why I wasn't able to pay attention during long meetings or why I wasn't able to manage some daily tasks. I frequently forgot appointments whenever I was engaged in something that interested me. I've since learned that when I'm deep into something I'm passionate about, I can sustain energy and enthusiasm far beyond what some people consider "normal." I've learned to align myself with projects, jobs, and purposes that I'm passionate about and to say a loving "no" to that which does not line up.

*"I guess I'd define passion as what
you choose to do when you don't
have to do it—the thing you enjoy so
much you're compelled to do it."*
~ **Dorie Clark, author of**
Reinventing You

Passion in Alignment

"When what you do is in alignment with who you are, you get energy from doing it," Suzanne Fetting, a Confidence Coach, told me. When you are aligned with your passions, coincidences and other signs will appear on the path. The key is to pay attention and be open to the extraordinary incidences, happenings, and experiences that show up. This is called synchronicity. One of my favorite authors, Dr. Wayne Dyer, explains synchronicity in this way:

> If it excites you, the very presence of that inner excitement is all the evidence you need to remind you that you're aligned with your true essence. When you are following your bliss, you are most amenable to receiving guidance from the spiritual realm. This is called synchronicity, a state in which you almost feel as if you are in a collaborative arrangement with fate.

My husband Joe and I were fortunate to attend one of Wayne's events before he passed away. It all began with a simple question, "Do you want to go to a Wayne Dyer event with me?" My husband recalled watching one of Wayne's shows on PBS and he liked learning from him.

So we planned to attend Wayne's event and celebrate our twenty-fifth anniversary in California.

Just before the event, one of Wayne's newsletters arrived in my email box. In it, he wrote this about passion:

> Passion always trumps excuses. Keep in mind that when I use the word passion, I'm not referring to the romantic notions that this concept conjures. Instead, I'm equating it to a vigorous kind of enthusiasm that you feel deep within you and that isn't easy to explain or define. This kind of passion propels you in a direction that seems motivated by a force beyond your control. It's the inner excitement of being on the right path, doing what feels good to you, and what you know you were meant to do.

After Wayne's event, Joe and I took off for Venice Beach to celebrate our anniversary. We wanted to stay in Santa Monica, but we ended up finding a deal at a vintage hotel.

"There must be a reason why we ended up here," I said.

Why in the world has my intuition led me to pick this hotel? I wondered. I had reviewed several hotels, received recommendations for Santa Monica hotels from friends–and here we were—in an area more suited for the casual, freewheeling lifestyle.

"It's getting late," Joe said. "Let's make the best of it."

The 100-year old hotel was charming. The staff was friendly and welcoming. After we unloaded our luggage, we took off to explore the ocean walk. To commemorate our special occasion, we wanted to watch a sunset on the beach.

The energy was high (pun intended, considering the marijuana we smelled here and there.) Color and movement were everywhere. A young man came bounding up, complimented me on how "fine" I looked, and attempted to sell me a CD. The sun was beginning to hang low in the sky, so Joe and I grabbed some beach chairs from the hotel and took off to watch the sunset.

Just as the last of the light began to fade, a man walked up to us.

"Hi! I'm sorry to bother you, but I saw you taking pictures and I don't have my phone with me. I wonder if you could send me some of your pictures?"

We were happy to share the photos, and after we sent them off, we began to talk. Francis was a psychotherapist from Boston. The topics of spirituality, theology, and yoga came up in our conversation. We told him we were celebrating our upcoming twenty-fifth anniversary and shared a bit about our night with Wayne Dyer. Soon it became too dark to talk, so we folded up our chairs and hugged goodbye.

When we arrived back at the hotel, we returned the beach chairs and struck up a conversation with the hotel manager. He gave us some history about the hotel and showed us pictures of the renovations that had taken place.

Just as we were about to head up to our room, a woman breezed in. As she put down her luggage, I spied a bright blue bag with the words, "I Can Do It." We had the same bag in our room.

"Were you at the Wayne Dyer event in Pasadena Friday night?" I asked.

"I was! I think I saw you there!" she said.

Beverly had come from London to attend the weekend event to explore her purpose and future. It was the perfect time for her since she was no longer working and she was seeking clarity and meaning for her next step. We laughed at the synchronicity that brought us all to the same place. After all, what are the chances of three people among 3,000 attendees ending up at the same hotel miles away from the event, at the exact same moment, with one arriving and the other leaving?

When we arrived back in our room, a text from Francis popped up. As I read his text, suddenly all the dots of the journey connected. He sent us a heartfelt poem, "A Blessing for Marriage" by John O'Donohue.

It was a beautiful twenty-fifth anniversary, and looking back, I could see all the moments of synchronicity that tied it all together and ended in an extraordinary experience.

That's the beauty of what happens in life when you are aligned with passion and purpose—things will fall into place. Moments of synchronicity and alignment will appear when you are on a path of joy.

Setting Intentions

Remember, people will come into your life and help guide you when you are on a passionate path. When I decided to become a speaker, I spent some time researching the best speakers. One name continually came up: Chad Hymas. I was familiar with Chad's story from Kevin Hall's book, *Aspire*. Chad became paralyzed from a bale of hay that landed on him at the age of twenty-seven. He turned his gift of gab into a successful speaking business—traveling over 200 days per year to speak at major corporations and conferences. I set an intention to meet Chad.

A few months later, I received an email notification that Chad would be coming to the Chicago area the next day. I contacted Chad's office to see whether it would be possible to meet him.

"Yes," was the response. I could meet with him briefly after his speaking gig.

I was six hours away at an event that I was working at and had planned to leave the next day. Instead, late at night, I hopped in my rental car and set out for home. Two hours into the drive, my tire blew. It was another hour and half before I could get back on the road again. I was dead tired and I still had another four hours of driving ahead of me. Yet, I was so passionately excited about meeting Chad that I willingly powered through the drive. Chad was in the Speaker Hall of

Fame and he was an immensely popular speaker—I wasn't going to miss this chance to meet him.

When I arrived at the hotel, I met with Chad in his room. Now before you get any crazy ideas, I should explain that Chad cannot control his body temperature. He was feeling dangerously cold that morning and was sitting in bed parked next to a heater.

During the next hour, we talked and connected. Chad gave me so many wonderful speaking tips and lots of advice. I could feel my confidence growing by the minute—I could do this speaking thing! Suddenly, Chad stopped and said, "Now I know why my other speaking trip didn't work out—we were supposed to meet."

Synchronicity in action.

Chad was set to go out of the country to speak, but when he arrived at the airport, he discovered he didn't have the proper visa for the trip. He turned around and went back home. Then he received a call from a friend asking him to take over a speaking gig in Chicago.

And that's how we met.

And that's how I started my speaking journey—powered by Chad's wisdom and advice.

When you are clear about what you want and passionate about your life—people will show up to open doors for you and guide you along the way.

Try it.

And stay open to the people and opportunities that show up on your path.

"Passion is what motivates you to wake up in the morning; it's an internal compass that drives your decision making. Passion is dedicating your life to something. It's not a passing fling where you devote lots of time and jump in fast in the beginning only to get burnt out and abandon it later. It's something you can't disconnect from. It's always there like a constant hunger. Passion is a gift from God."
~ Julie Seawright, sign language interpreter

Giving Ourselves Permission to Play

Do you remember your early days of being a kid without a care in the world? Do you remember the feelings of excitement and anticipation when you were little?

When I close my eyes, I can remember the swings at a park near my home. I spent so many hours at this park as a very young girl. I can still feel the warmth of the sun as I reached the peak of the upswing and how it felt to stay suspended in mid-air for a fraction of a second before beginning the downswing.

Something so simple—swinging on a swing—yet it represents everything I know about passion: carefree joy and freedom.

And here's the thing: We can get that back at any age. It all begins with the power to choose our thoughts and our attitudes. We can infuse playfulness into our lives by our actions as well.

Let me introduce you to someone who chose to play like a kid again. Theresa Rose has a passion for hula hoops. Ever since she was a young girl, she loved dancing, but as a woman carrying a few extra pounds, she never gave herself permission to indulge in it. One day, she went to a summer solstice celebration and watched a dancer using a hula hoop. "That was the first time I saw a person dancing without fear and without a male partner," Theresa said.

She then felt encouraged to purchase a hula hoop, but she rarely touched it. A few years and many pounds later, Theresa realized she was putting life on hold. She had become quite sedentary and depressed. There was no spark in her daily activities.

Theresa picked up the hula hoop again, but this time, she fell in love. She named the hoop, "Stella," and Theresa finally gave herself permission to play. She dove deep into hula-hoop dancing and discovered an incredible joy that resulted from her newfound playtime.

"I'm a strong advocate of abandoning exercise and embracing play," Theresa explained. "When you start moving physically and give yourself permission to play, it re-frames your mind to be open to receiving joy daily."

Theresa went on to explain how passion fits in with play:

Passion means unbridled enthusiasm from within—it can't be manipulated, it can't be held, it can't be controlled. It's like a language that you speak—when you first start, you might not know all the language. We are exposed to a language we already know inside; we become more familiar and explore that language—it becomes second nature and that's the only language you want to speak. When you find people in the same passion, the same language, some amazing things happen for business or relationships in the community. So it's wonderful to know what your passion is and let your passion guide your daily activities and guide your decisions. Passion is a really strong energy—people will feel it.

Theresa now shares her passion with others, teaching them how to incorporate play into their lives and connect with their passions. She has a collapsible hoop that she brings on the plane with her, and every single day, she taps into her mental and physical energy by stepping into a hoop and letting it fly.

So let's stop here for a moment and reflect back on moments in your life when you were engaged in joyous play. Jot down your memories.

When was the last time you engaged in carefree, joyous play? What can you do today to experience play once again?

_____

_____

_____

_____

_____

_____

"*Passion—the hunger, the drive, the love, the fire in the belly—is key in the achievements of any person engaged in any endeavor. Passion is fuel for success. If you don't have it, you need to keep looking for something to get passionate about. When you don't enjoy what you're doing, you work more slowly, less efficiently, less creatively, and people with more positive energy pass you by. Nothing great in life has ever been done without a little passion.*"

~ Ivan Misner and Don Morgan,
Masters of Success

CHAPTER 3

Finding Your Passion, or Not?

"Once you find your passion, you
will love doing what you need
to do to achieve it, while many
others without passion will not be
successful because they either do not
apply their talents or quit. Without
passion, you will lack the direction
and focus that are necessary if you
are to succeed."

~ Don M. Green

The Question We Always Ask Kids

"What do you want to be when you grow up?"

I can remember this question from elementary school. I remember the usual answers from the class: fireman, teacher, policeman, garbage man (the kid's father had that job), pilot, hairdresser (yeah, I'm dating myself with that term), and so on.

I just wanted to be a mom, just like my own mother. She was my role model and she did it well. I wanted to stay home, have a bunch of kids, and be a mom. But I was afraid no one else would think that was a goal so I didn't say anything about just wanting to be a mom. I don't remember what I even said in the classroom—I think I said I wanted to be a teacher.

Years later, my first child was born. For two months, I dropped him off at a friend's house and went off to work. My mind wasn't on my work—I no longer had a passion for the job. I wanted to be a mom every minute of the day. My heart was calling out for that path.

I didn't care what it would take to live on one income as I was willing to live in a teepee if that's what it came down to. I gave two-weeks' notice at my job and became an at-home mom.

"Passion means inner motivation and desire—it makes you get up in the morning and you feel fired up to invest your best energy throughout your day."
~ **Terry Hadaway,** *Live Your Why*

Terry Hadaway, author of *Live Your Why*, says that we have the question all wrong. Instead of asking "What do you want to be?" we should be asking, "How do you want to live?"

That's right. How?

The question of how we want to live changes everything. It redirects the focus from "what" we want to be to "how" we want to live our lives. It also opens us up to design a life of meaning, instead of a life defined around a job title.

"This takes things to a whole new level," Terry writes. "The job is no longer the point; it is the means to living a life that matters. That's exactly what people today are seeking."

For a long time, Terry thought he was living a life that mattered through his educational ministry work. He left a large mega-church to work in a small church in Alabama, seeking more simplicity in life. Terry ghostwrites books for authors like Billy Graham, Max Lucado, John MacArthur, Charles Stanley, Sheila Walsh, Chuck Swindoll, John Maxwell, and Ken Blanchard. Yet, despite the work he was doing, there was still an emptiness inside. He wanted something more, but he didn't know what "more" was.

After a bit of soul searching and using Dan Miller's book, *48 Days to the Work You Love*, Terry realized he was happiest when he was continually using his creativity. Today, his passion for learning and leading eventually led him to a career in higher education at a medical college where he is the Assistant Director of Academic Computing and an Assistant Professor in the Medical Education Department.

"Passion means inner motivation and desire—passion makes you get up in the morning and you feel fired up to invest your best energy. When it comes to passion, you can't make yourself stop thinking about it," Terry explains. "When you get up each day and live your why, you are indeed wealthy."

What Are You Willing to Change to Have a Passionate Life?

I become excited when I meet someone and he or she says, "I love what I do." Those are the people who are on a path of purpose with their lives. If I ask, "So what would you be doing if you weren't doing this?" and they say with complete passion, "I can't imagine doing anything else," that's how I know they're living their joy. Life is "on" for them.

Tell me, what about you—can you answer honestly and say you love what you do each day? Do you wake up each morning in anticipation of being able to enjoy the day ahead?

If the answer is no, don't despair. At any given moment in your life, you can begin again in a new direction. You always, always, always have the option to take action—whether by changing thoughts, attitudes, or actions.

When I go to a party and meet up with people I haven't seen in years—and there's absolutely nothing new with them—this makes me sad. Their kids are little older, they've had a vacation or two, but everything else in their lives is absolutely the same old, same old.

Don't let that be you.

You can choose joy. You can choose to be happy. You can choose in favor of your passions.

I'm often challenged by people who claim they have no passion in their life or they have no idea what their passions are. They feel stuck right where they are.

If this is you, here's what I tell others:

You can choose to CHANGE SOMETHING, or choose to stay in the same situation.

What are you willing to change to experience the full height of joy in your life? What are you willing to give up so that you can invite what you truly want into your life? Take a minute to answer those questions with complete, raw, honesty.

What are you willing to change?

_____

_____

_____

_____

_____

_____

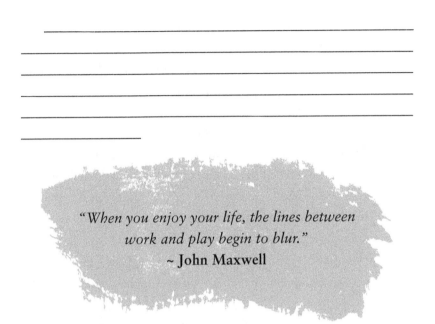

"When you enjoy your life, the lines between work and play begin to blur."
~ **John Maxwell**

When Your Job Crushes Your Soul

Joel Boggess was wrapped up in a "soul-crushing" job. He snagged a cushy job with Morgan Stanley, a job he thought he wanted when he put himself through college for a second Master's degree. At first, the spoils of success were thrilling: nice suits, rich food, and a snazzy car to drive. Joel spent the days in long meetings, wheeling and dealing in investments. The evenings were devoted to networking and meeting potential clients. But when Joel arrived home, he didn't have much energy left in him. His wife was last on the daily list of things to attend to. Yes, the money was fabulous, but he woke up each day feeling as if someone were squeezing the life out of him. Every morning, Joel started his day by putting on those elegant suits and a tie—but as time went on, the knotted tie began to feel like a noose around his neck.

This was supposed to be his "dream" job, the one he envisioned when he racked up the Master's in Counseling and the MBA. Even after putting the initials behind his name, Joel learned that higher education doesn't necessarily translate into higher salaries, but it definitely translates into a higher responsibility level. When I interviewed him, Joel told me, "If you want to be a doctor, say a brain surgeon or a lawyer, yeah, that requires a higher education and you want a person with a higher education in that job," says Joel. "But in other jobs, it's a myth that higher education will guarantee the highest position and salary. We've all been taught to stay in school, to continue to study. College freshmen, by the time they graduate, 80 percent of what they learn will be obsolete. I made the mistake, unfortunately, that many people make: thinking higher education equals more opportunity," Joel explains. "I found out very quickly that it was a disappointment. I thought if I put it on my resume, like a magic wand, people would beat down my door offering me jobs."

The money was nice, but the corporate job was slowly killing Joel's spirit. His wife urged him to leave his job. "There were a few aspects of being in corporate America that I liked, but it wasn't feeding my spirit," said Joel. "I recognized it more and more every day. With a lot of prayer and discussions with my wife, I knew I needed to do something that was more me."

One morning, Joel woke up and he had a difficult time getting out of bed. What happened to the happy, passionate guy he used to be, he wondered.

Joel knew he wanted something more, but he didn't know how to define "more."

So Joel began by looking for clues in his past. Joel specifically asked himself some questions:

- What are my skills?
- What were the moments in my life when I felt fulfilled?
- What brings me joy?

- What makes my heart sing?

Joel looked back on his life and started seeing a pattern with his skills and gifts. Back in high school in San Antonio, Joel taught karate to adults after school. He did more than just teaching the mechanics of how to perform the sport; he found himself teaching in a way that incorporated spiritual, mental, and emotional growth. His students were flourishing in holistic ways. He did the same when he became a lifeguard after high school and taught swimming classes. "I did a lot more than teaching the strokes," Joel says. "I helped build up confidence and self-esteem and helped them go to a better place in their lives." Joel also worked as a personal trainer after high school, and he found joy in helping others achieve their goals.

As Joel looked back on his skills, he realized one of his gifts was the ability to work with people and coach them. His wife introduced him to Dan Miller's 48 Day Coaching program[1] and urged him to look into it. "My wife knew I was frustrated and I wasn't 100 percent there. She wanted me to experience meaning and fulfillment." Joel realized his wife was right; he wanted something more out of life than just a job. All the signs pointed to life coaching. He made up his mind to leave his job and pursue the very thing that was calling out within him: to help others find their own paths to fulfillment.

The day Joel left his job, he experienced a total life change. His first thought upon waking up was *freedom!* That was the last day Joel wore a suit and a tie. The next day, he woke up with unbridled enthusiasm and began to put the pieces of the puzzle together that would form his coaching business. "I surrounded myself with successful people," he said. "I hung with people who were already gathering six figures or more in their businesses, and I modeled my business after theirs. I used their materials—I didn't see any reason to reinvent the wheel. I created my

---

1   Visit www.48days.com for more information.

style and my flair, but I used what was already working. As I grew my business and grew myself as a coach, I added my own flavor."

Today, Joel continues to reinvent himself, and his wife, Pei, has joined him in the process by selling her dental practice. Together, they created a successful podcast show, *ReLaunch*, which features people who have changed directions on the journey of life to discover their true calling.

"If people understand their gifts, their skills and abilities, and understand their personal style, they learn to embrace their natural ability. They let down their guard. They stop trying to become somebody else," Joel said. "I sincerely believe we are all created with a purpose and we all have a responsibility to find out what that is and to understand who we are. When we are in touch with our best features and qualities, our responsibility is to pursue that with passion."

> *"To be what we are and to become what we are capable of becoming is the only end in life."*
> ~ **Robert Louis Stevenson**

Feeling Stuck

I don't know what I want to do.

I don't know what I'm passionate about.

I don't have a passion.

If those are your responses to the question, "What are you passionate about?" it's a sign you're playing safe. If safe is what you want, then you know exactly where you're going and you won't need a map to get there.

Life will be much of the same year after year with this approach. You might as well put this book down and call it a day because there won't be much need to read through the rest of the chapters.

The comfortable zone is a nice, cozy, safe place to be. Some people love it there. They're perfectly content with going through life each day in the same way. Live. Rinse. Repeat.

I know you're not one to settle for mediocrity or you wouldn't have picked up this book to read.

> *"I define passion as any pursuit or interest*
> *that makes your heart race or makes you*
> *feel like time is not measurable anymore,*
> *or that makes you feel like you have a*
> *reward for doing it."*
> ~ **Chris Brogan**

Incorporating Your Passion into Your Work

Way back in the early days of blogging and social media, I met Chris Brogan at a social media conference in Chicago. Chris quickly became known as the go-to guy for social media and business, working with corporations like Disney, Coke, Google, and Sony (to name just a few). Tony Robbins featured Chris in his Internet Money Masters series. Chris interviewed Richard Branson for the cover story in *Success Magazine*. His books are *New York Times* bestsellers. He has been on the Dr. Phil Show and MSNBC.

And Chris is one of the nicest, kindest, most down-to-earth guys I've ever met.

From a young age, Chris Brogan was into comic books and superheroes. His grandfather was a candy salesman, who would often take Chris on his rounds. Instead of begging for candy, Chris asked for comic books. Every time he obtained a new comic book, his heart would race at the anticipation of sitting down to read and time would simply fade away. As a young kid, Chris had dreams of becoming a superhero comic book author, but as an adult, his path took him through the corporate world of telecommunications for eighteen years.

Chris' interest in comic books never faded. Instead, he found ways to incorporate his passion for superheroes into parts of his work. Speaking. Books. Blog posts. Social media. In many aspects of his life and work, you can find tales and lessons of superheroes woven in.

"We can take pieces of our passion and turn it into something useful," Chris said. "Sometimes our dream doesn't immediately match our business—sometimes we look closer and we can see connecting points and we can make one fit another. It doesn't mean that we have to ignore our childhood passions, but find ways to implement them in our lives today."

I love what Chris shared. It's brilliant, actually. If your work isn't currently something you're passionate about, what are some ways you could incorporate your passion for something into your current work?

Not too long ago, I spoke at a corporation that handled medical transportation calls. There's not a lot of room for fun there since employees are tethered to their work stations for most of the day. Yet one employee frequently shares her passion for cake decorating by bringing in different cakes for everyone to enjoy. Many of the employees also hire her to make cakes for their special events.

"Take your passion and serve others with it," is advice that comes up again and again among the people I've interviewed for this book.

"In my experience, I've seen so many people who don't know what their passion is or where to serve," Chris shared. "In most situations, we've never really had the right exposures to the right catalyst that would make it work for us. We interact in very linear ways, and we don't get to see what may be exciting to us. One way to find that or expose passion is to become more open to many adventures, childish whims, and other opportunities for random experience—and then go forward from there."

Chris tells me we certainly can live our lives without passion—that we can go from birth to death without passion and live *some* kind of life—but that's like ordering cheese pizza all our lives. We have so many other opportunities for pizza, or finding passion, so why not choose passion?

"Sometimes people think passion is frivolous or maybe a luxury," Chris said. "But I think it's a gift and an opportunity."

During a Smart Passive Income podcast by Pat Flynn, my eyes perked up (I was reading through a transcript) when Pat's guest Joel Comm, an entrepreneur who specializes in Internet businesses, shared his thoughts on passion:

> I would just really encourage people to figure out what that thing is that they do so—that they're so passionate about that they would do it even if they weren't getting paid for it. Life is short and I believe that every person is created by God with unique passions, talents, skills, abilities, and personality that make us so special that only we as individuals can bring that specific value to the world around us. And that's what we're here for. It's not about us. It's about how we can be vessels that can be used to enrich other people's lives.
>
> And if you do that, the money is going to come. So figure out what that thing is that really sets you on fire, that fire in your

belly that makes you burn to do that thing. And then find a way to do it. Even if you can only do it a little bit for now as you work on your job or getting financially on your feet. Do that thing because it's going to be life-giving for you as you do it, and it's going to be life-giving for the people whose lives you touched. And it's a cycle that's just keeps going round and round. It feeds. It's kind of like love. When you give love, you get love. And it's something you never run out of. So whatever that thing is you love to do, give it out and it will come back around.

I read Joel's words over and over. Money is often the number one factor that holds people back from truly living their dreams. And we've got it all backwards—we aim for the money in hopes that money will bring us the joy and happiness we're waiting for all along.

The Top Five Traits of Passionate People

In the process of studying passion over several years, I interviewed over 200 people for this book. Not all of their stories have made it into the book, but what I discovered is that the people who are deep into passionate living share some common traits.

The good news is this: All of these traits can be acquired by changing thoughts, attitudes, and actions. Here are the top five common traits I found in passionate people:

1. **Authenticity:** Passionate people know who they are and what they want. They have something to strive for: goals, dreams, plans. They can articulate their passions to others. They continually choose in favor of their passions. They recognize their talents and they share them freely with others.

2. **Open-Mindedness:** Passionate people begin with a beginner's mind, and they have an intense desire, openness, and willingness

to learn. They are creative when it comes to ways to get what they want and need.

3. **Self-Drive:** Passionate people will go above and beyond for something they believe in. They are disciplined and focused when it comes to something they're passionate about. They seek out and engage with others who are in alignment with them.

4. **High Energy:** Passion is energy, and when you're engaged in something that you're passionate about, your energy level is above average. Passion and enthusiasm are entwined.

5. **Resilience:** The ability to bounce back is a valuable trait that determines the longevity of staying engaged in a passionate life. "The Bounce Factor" is different in everyone, but when you are driven by passion and purpose, you are less likely to give up and walk away when faced with obstacles. Passionate people are willing to fail. They are persistent and, sometimes, relentless. The other word associated with this trait: grit.

In every interview with people who are living passionately, I saw the same five traits in every one of them. Some displayed those traits as young children. Others developed those traits on their journey.

Here are some questions to ask yourself when you are exploring your passions:

- Am I being authentic? Is this for me?
- Am I approaching this with an open mind? Am I willing to learn?
- Am I willing to sustain this on my own?
- Am I being internally (from within) or externally (by others) driven?
- Does this give me energy?
- Am I easily frustrated by this? Am I giving up too easily? What will it take to persist? Do I want to persist?

CHAPTER 4

Discovering the Passion Spark

"If there is no passion in your life, then have you really lived? Find your passion, whatever it may be. Become it, and let it become you and you will find great things happen for you, to you, and because of you."
~ T. Alan Armstrong

f you've done the same thing day in and day out for years, then you've created a comfort zone you're familiar with. There's a quote by John Maxwell that says it well: "Being in your comfort zone may feel good, but it leads to mediocrity and, therefore, dissatisfaction." When you make the decision to dive into a passion, you're going to stretch yourself in ways you've never been stretched before. You're going to push your body, your mind, and your soul into a whole new stratosphere. You're going to be very uncomfortable at times, but if you push yourself through it with your passion straight ahead of you, you'll arrive in places you never imagined.

The Two Choices You Have

When it comes to living life, you have two choices:

1. Letting life happen to you, or
2. Making life happen.

The second one requires some thought and planning. John Maxwell, in his book, *The 15 Invaluable Laws of Growth*, says, "Most people allow their lives to simply happen to them. They float along. They wait. They react. And by the time a large portion of their life is behind them, they realize they should have been more proactive and strategic."

In every one of the interviews I conducted for this book, the very first step that everyone took was simply to become clear about their passion. We already have the answers within us, but we often don't make the time or take the proper action to allow them to surface. Clarity is the first step. You must understand and feel the emotion of passion when figuring out what brings you joy.

> *"Look in your own heart. Unless I'm crazy, right now a still, small voice is piping up, telling you as it has ten thousand times, the calling that is yours and yours alone.*
> ~ **Steven Pressfield,** *The War of Art*

So let's stop here for a minute and put that clarity in writing.

I want you to picture an absolutely amazing life that is unique just for you. What would it look like? How would you spend your days? Where would you live? How would you live? What would you have? Who would you be with?

Take a moment to close your eyes and let the answers to those questions come to you. Download a worksheet here: agelesspassions. com/PASSIONBookInsider

The possibilities are endless.

So why do we trip ourselves up when it comes to dreaming, thinking, and manifesting what we're truly passionate about?

Because there's a lot that gets in our way.

For one thing, the voices in our heads often drown out the calling in our hearts. It's all too easy to rationalize your passion and your dreams away. There's not enough time, money, skills, experience, this or that. Many of the obstacles we simply create in our heads—and then we stop the whole process toward achieving our dreams before we can even start.

Thomas L. Friedman, *New York Times* foreign affairs columnist and author of *The World Is Flat*, offers the following advice for how to create a plan and make it work:

So whatever you plan to do, whether you plan to travel the world, go to grad school, join the workforce, or take some time off to think, don't just listen to your head. Listen to your heart. It's the best career counselor there is. Do what you really love to do, and if you don't know what that is yet, well, keep searching because if you find it, you'll bring that something extra to your work.

"All we are is the result of what we have thought."
~ **Buddha**

It's very easy to become frustrated in the "pursuit of passion" and to feel that you continually come up short if you've not discovered the one big thing you're passionate about. That's why I love the Passion Test so much—it's simple, it's direct, and it gets right to the heart of what is meaningful in your life. A little later, I'm going to share more about this test—so hang tight!

One of the first steps on the journey to passion is to get rid of the old ways of thinking that brought you to where you are now. If you want to reject a new way of thinking, you will remain stuck in the same old, same old life.

Passion is an energy just like love. And just like love, it comes in all different dimensions. It's comfortable like the love you have for your mother, but it's also the hot, heart-throbbing, mind-blowing feeling that you have for someone special in your life.

I hear excuses from people all the time about why they can't pursue their passions. I admit I trip myself up over them too. "I don't have the time, money, energy, or resources to do what I passionately want to do," people tell me. The concept is simple: If you focus on what you're passionate about, everything expands. If you focus on the negative, the lack, the stuff that's *not* working, all you're going to get is more of that. If you spend your time watching TV instead of doing something that puts you on the path to your passion, that's a choice you are making with your attention. The next thing you know, five years have passed by and you're still not living your dreams.

From the moment you wake up, you're faced with decisions about how your day will unfold. How will you use your time? Whom will you surround yourself with? What attitude will you choose?

You may feel powerlessly stuck with your job, your home life, and your situation, but the reality is, you are giving your power away by remaining "stuck." When you feel that life has plateaued, it is a sign that something must be changed. With every choice you make, you are either moving in the direction you truly want, or further away from it.

My own path to passion was shaped by Janet Attwood, co-author of *The Passion Test: The Effortless Path to Discovering Your Life Purpose*: I picked up her book on the recommendation of a friend.

Janet is a transformational speaker who has given the Passion Test to hundreds of thousands of people worldwide, including The Dalai Lama, Stephen Covey, Sir Richard Branson, T. Harv Eker, and Jack Canfield. For her passionate work with kids in detention and homeless people, Janet received the President's Service Award.

I signed up for a one-day workshop with Janet in Chicago. The day before, a friend invited me to a private gathering with Janet in her home.

I had a dilemma; I was serving on a committee for a fundraiser and the fundraiser was the same night. I sat there, completely torn in two. What to do?

I had *The Passion Test* in my hand and I looked through the pages. I needed some guidance and I found it: "Whenever you're faced with a choice, decision, or an opportunity, always choose in favor of your passions."

My heart wasn't in the fundraiser—I was doing it out of an obligation for a friend. This passion stuff—wow, it made my heart sing! I wanted to meet Janet, I wanted to learn more about passion, and I wanted a passionate life!

When you choose in favor of your passions, amazing things happen. Not only did I meet Janet that night, my life simply took an incredibly passionate path with her mentorship.

When I first did The Passion Test, I struggled with my answers. I kept resorting to safe, cute little things that really didn't reflect what was in my heart at the time. I kept encountering excuses and feelings of disbelief that were blocking me from dreaming about what I really wanted to invite into my life.

"Don't focus on the how; focus on the what," Janet instructed. "Once you know the what, the how will take care of itself."

So I tackled the Passion Test again, this time with gusto, and after finishing the test, my ultimate, number one passion was simple:

I wanted to barefoot water ski year-round.

So, of course, the first things that popped into my mind were all the obstacles:

- The lakes are frozen in Chicago during the winter.
- I don't have anyone to barefoot with locally.
- I don't own a barefoot boat.
- I don't have the money to barefoot water ski year-round.

But Janet's words echoed once again:

"Focus on the what. The how will take care of itself."

Okay then, I had nothing to lose....

When January rolled around, I took off to Florida to write a book with Keith St. Onge, the World Barefoot Champion. So, of course, I spent a few days on the water barefoot water skiing.

In February, I went back to Florida to do a filming for Growing Bolder TV, a segment that was later shown on over 100 PBS stations and cable TV.

In March, I received a bonus from work and spent a weekend barefooting with some gals.

And so it went.

The more I shared my passion on Facebook, the more I began to attract other barefoot water skiers, and they invited me to barefoot water ski with them all over the U.S. The first time I jumped in a boat with people I didn't know, my husband wasn't too happy, but he relaxed once he saw how much joy I came home with after a great skiing session.

By the time November rolled around, I had barefoot water skied every month but April. *Not too bad*, I figured. But it wasn't over...in December, I received an invitation to barefoot once again. In Wisconsin. For a charity event. In forty-four-degree water.

I happily said yes.

So for that entire year, I barefoot water skied eleven months out of the twelve!

That's why it's so important to identify what you truly want to bring into your life. What you focus on, expands. Without clarity, we tend to drift through life until one day, we have no more life to drift through.

For more information on The Passion Test, visit www.agelesspassions.com/PASSIONbookinsider.

> *"When you are really happy doing something, there's a hint of what you are passionate about right there."*
> ~ Singyin Lee

Say Yes to Success

Before I met Janet Attwood, I met Debra Poneman. The two of them are great friends and soul sisters. You met each of them in the foreword.

At Debra's *Yes to Success* workshop, I created my very first vision board—and it's a board that I've continually updated. Many of the things I first visualized became part of my life over the last few years.

Debra's journey down the road of success took a few winding turns. She taught meditation for many years and then turned to a job in finance, thinking that money would be the answer to her dreams. One day, she signed up for a workshop that would change her life.

"I thought the workshop would be about stocks and bonds, but when I arrived, it was about how your mind creates your reality and how if you think about success and prosperity, you will draw success and prosperity to you," Debra said. "If you are always complaining about how broke you are and that there's no way you can be successful in your chosen field, you will draw lack and struggle to you. That's the first time I heard that we can attract what we think about."

The next morning, Debra quit her job. She began studying the Masters of Success—Napoleon Hill, Catherine Ponder, Florence Scovel Shinn, Wallace D. Wattles—and learned the principles they each followed. She noticed common lessons from each of them. From this, she launched her very first "Yes to Success" workshop. She was flat broke and certainly not successful by any means, but she had a deep desire to achieve success through her workshops.

The 100 List

During her Yes to Success workshop, Debra introduced me to the "100 List."

It's your personal list of 100 things to do, be, or have in your lifetime. Some will recognize this as a Bucket List. I prefer to call it a Life List. What's on your Life List? If you don't have one, go to www.agelesspassions.com/PASSIONbookinsider to download your free list.

At first, I had difficulty even coming up with twenty-five things to list. My mind kept going into that place of what I call "Yeah, right."

You know what I mean?

- Yeah, right, there's no way I can...
- Yeah, right, there's no way I will...
- Yeah, right, there's no way I'll have...

Stop right there.

You're already blocking yourself. I know because I did just that when I first attempted to clarify what I wanted in life.

During a break at the workshop, I spied a Chicken Soup for the Soul book on a display table. I love the Chicken Soup for the Soul stories. Many years ago, I dreamed about having a chapter in one. And now I really wanted a chapter in a Chicken Soup for the Soul book! I added it to my 100 List.

Many weeks later, I was going over my 100 List/Life List and realized that I had not done a single thing toward that item on the list. How in the world was I going to become a Chicken Soup for the Soul author if I never submitted anything for the editors to consider?

Right then and there, I went online to find out how I could submit a story. I shut off my phone, closed my office door, and wrote. Two hours later, I was satisfied with my essay and submitted it to the Chicken Soup for the Soul site.

Then I forgot about it.

A few weeks later, I received an email. My essay was being considered for the "Finding Your Happiness" edition.

Boy, was I happy!

Once the confirmation email came in and the final edits were done, I eagerly waited for the box of books to arrive. No words can describe the feeling I felt when I pulled the first of ten books out of the box.

When it comes to creating a life you love, your job is not to focus on the how, but the what. So let's do a mini-exercise here:

If life were truly ideal, what would you be experiencing?

_____

_____

_____

_____

_____

_____

_____

If life were truly ideal, what would you have?

_____

_____

_____

_____

_____

_____

If life were truly ideal, what would you be doing?

_____

_____

_____

_____

_____

_____

_____

If life were truly ideal, how would you be feeling?

_____

_____

_____

_____

_____

_____

Your answers to the questions above reflect what's truly in your heart. For even more clarity and to identify your top five passions, that's where the Passion Test comes into play. You'll find more information about the Passion Test and other downloads at: www.agelesspassions.com/PASSIONbookinsider

"Chase down your passion like it's the last bus of the night."
~ Terri Guillemets

The Three Clues to Your Passions

I used to be so envious of people who found their passions early in life and went on to have stellar careers in that direction. For many years, I was drifting through life with a couple of minor dreams, waiting for that magical "Someday" to appear so I could start living them.

- Someday I was going to write a book.
- Someday I was going to travel.
- Someday I was going to get up on stage and speak.
- Someday I was going to buy a boat.
- Someday I was going to live my passions—if I just knew what they were....

It wasn't until my forty-fourth birthday that I started looking for some clues to my passions. Here's what I came up with:

- I love to write.
- I love to talk to people.
- I love to entertain people.
- I love nature, especially sunsets and water.
- I love being alone. (Yeah, the introverted extrovert...)
- I love helping others.

The more I thought about it, the more I began to realize the inklings of passion were indeed there. I just had ignored them for so long. There are three places you can look to find clues to your passions: the past, present, and future. For the next exercise, you'll need a blank notebook, a really good pen, and at least an hour of uninterrupted time. Turn the phone off, turn the computer off, and go to a place that is comfortable and private. Now we're going to visit three different scenarios:

Past

Think back to your childhood days. Go back to a time when your days were filled with something you truly enjoyed doing.

Where were you at?

Who were you with?

What did you long for as a child?

What did you grow up dreaming about?

What were your moments of joy?

What skills did you use?

What were you good or great at doing?

What have you abandoned doing but wish you could do again?

Present

The present day is filled with great clues—yet, we often go through daily routines without truly understanding our thoughts and our desires. Pay attention to the moments during the day when your mind wanders to something you'd rather be doing.

Where do you often go in your mind with your thoughts?

What do you daydream about?

When you are doing something that is of no interest to you, where do your thoughts drift off to?

Where do you wish you could be right now?

What do you wish you could do right now?

Whom do you wish you could hang around with?

Future

I call this part the "Someday" exercise, because it often involves the plans, goals, hopes, dreams, and desires that you've put off for some day. So let's dive right into it:

What are you putting off for "Someday?"

What are you putting off for when conditions are "ideal" or "perfect?"

What are the big dreams that you eventually hope to get to?

When you envision the future, whom are you with?

What are you doing in the future?

What do you have?

What have you accomplished?

How do others see you?

So what are you going to do with all of this once you've written it down? That remains up to you. Clarity without action still produces no results—you must take action to set the passion journey in motion.

"Passion, it lies in all of us, sleeping... waiting...and through unwanted...unbidden... it will stir...open its jaws and howl. It speaks to us...guides us...passion rules us all, and we obey. What other choice do we have?
~ Joss Whedon, screenwriter and director

Dean Landsman: A Passion for Radio

When Dean Landsman's father arrived home from work, he looked as if he went through a war—he walked in with a tired, haggard look. Three-year-old Dean's vision of work was associated with the unhappiness he saw on his father's face each day.

From that very young age, Dean was fascinated with radio and he loved listening to music while his mother ironed. At the end of a song, Dean recalled hearing the DJ announcing the next one. He noted how happy the guy sounded. That very moment sparked a passion and a career in radio.

As a teen, Dean researched everything he could about radio careers. He purchased three radios and listened to hosts, taking notes about news, advertisements, and contests.

Dean snagged a summer job working five days a week in the control room of a local radio station as a teen. Every day, he worked behind the scenes, wishing he could have the opportunity to be in front of the microphone.

One afternoon, the radio host became very sick. Just before rushing off to the bathroom, he asked Dean to step in and take over by introducing the weather and running tape.

"I called my mother and told her to turn on the radio just before I went on," Dean recalled. It was a defining moment for him; he knew without a doubt, radio was his passion.

"There was not a single doubt in my mind that I would pursue my passion in radio," Dean said. "When you're passionate about something, it's important to be persistent; the more you do something that you have a passion for, the more passion increases. Life itself is not perfect, even when following your passion, but passion begets passion—the more you have it, the more you get."

Dean went off to college, graduated with a degree in Radio and TV, and spent his career deep in all aspects of radio, including owning a radio station. By age forty, he had fulfilled many of his dreams, but the field was changing rapidly. Dean shifted paths, creating a consulting company. Today, he's deep into another passion: baseball.

*"I think you discover your passion
or your passion discovers you—you
never know when something will just
tap you."*
~ Dean Landsman

I love what Dean said: you discover your passion or your passion discovers you. This was also true for Chris Arceneaux who lived near a golf course while growing up. What began as a simple entrepreneurial idea turned into a burning passion for him.

Chris grew up in Lafayette, Louisiana, in a community that constantly battled crime and drugs. His father passed away when he was eleven years old, leaving his mother to raise six children on her own.

As a young child, Chris exercised his entrepreneurial skills by gathering up wayward golf balls from a nearby course, stuffing them into empty egg cartons and bookbags, and selling them to passing golfers on Louisiana Ave.

"One day, I was in tears picking up balls near the fence and grieving for my father. I watched the doctors and lawyers move through the course with smiles on their faces. I wanted to experience the same good life. At the same time, a policeman was arresting a juvenile nearby. I didn't want that to happen to me. So I ran to the fence and wondered what it was like on the other side," says Chris.

As the tears continued to flow, Chris threw up a silent prayer. "If you just give me a chance, I will get on the inside of the course."

Someday I'm going to have a golf bag with my name on it, Chris thought.

Not long after, Chris was mowing his neighbor's lawn and went into his neighbor's house for a glass of lemonade. He spied a golf club on the table and picked it up. After his neighbor paid him for the lawn service, he gave him the club and seven balls. Chris went home and practiced in his backyard. One of his long shots ended up breaking his neighbor's window.

"Golf was my passion the minute the club was in my hand," Chris said. "I felt free. That was my ticket out of the community. That grip was like lightning—chills in my bones and my pores—it felt magical and it was so electric."

Chris' uncle, along with two of his uncle's closest friends, took him to play 18-holes. As soon as Chris sat in the golf cart, he knew he wanted more. A passion for golf took hold of him. Both his uncle and neighbor mentored him, giving him advice, tips, and encouragement. As Chris improved his skills on the course, he began to dream of playing professionally. He was all set to go to college with a golf scholarship. Then his mother became ill, forcing Chris to walk away from his dream temporarily. Chris took a job at Walmart to help his mom cover the cost of living expenses.

Chris rapidly moved up the ranks at Walmart into management. He then took a sales job at a furniture store in Louisiana before moving to New York and working at a car dealership. He married his sweetheart and they worked seven days a week to make a living and for Chris to make a name for himself in New York.

Nevertheless, golf was still in his heart. He started cultivating his game—hitting a thousand balls a day. Chris joined the Amateur Tour and won eight events. He was named Player of the Year. He upped his game by finding sponsors and hitting the professional circuit. Through his career, he's won over eighty events.

"I'm living the dream," Chris said. "My boyhood dream escalated and I've been able to accomplish a laundry list of things on and off the golf course. I received the Key to the City to Lafayette, Louisiana, became an Ambassador for Mercedes Benz, and started a foundation in honor of my late father to help underprivileged kids get scholarships and learn life skills. My dream was so far from where I started as a little boy."

The Darby Foundation is Chris' way of giving back and inspiring young children to make positive choices. He mentors others the same way he himself was mentored as a young boy.

"Every day I discover who I am. God has created me to be a vessel to help others tap into their passion."

Here's what Chris has to say about passion:

Do we discover passion or does passion discover us? I think it works both ways. It's momentum. When I look back on my life, it's like a diving board, springing up and down. Sometimes I'm down, I think, "Why am I not receiving worldwide fame?" I bounce up. I want to be there. I have tears. I want to write the checks for those kids. I'm jumping on the diving board and I'm going down—when I can finally make that plunge, that's all the momentum that was building up—that splash is the passion. When we are moving to that unknown ahead of us—we are building that momentum on the diving board. We have that picture, but we can't see it—who God intended us to be, that's who we all are. We want to get to that place where God wants us to be, yet we haven't discovered it. Some people don't tap into that core. That passion is inside of us—that thing that keeps us fighting, keeps us living—we constantly have to be on that diving board bouncing, because some day we will make that splash, that BIG splash.

I believe we are constantly developing and conditioning our passions just like a muscle—to develop it, you're constantly conditioning that muscle to create the physique. You're constantly building those conditions. Our passion is a muscle, we have gifts and talents inside of us that we don't even know about, but they are there and it's like a light switch. Some people just stay with the light off, they're living with the off button. Passion is a muscle we constantly have to be pushing and building.

The name "Chris Arceneaux" stitched on the leather golf bag is an everyday reminder that passion is worth pursuing.

CHAPTER 5

Listening Within

> *"It doesn't interest me what you do for a living. I want to know what you ache for, and if you dream of meeting your heart's longing."*
> ~ Oriah Mountain Dreamer

"What do you see yourself doing five years from now?"

That's a standard interview question for corporate jobs. There are classes out there that will help you craft a tight, elevator-pitch answer that is generically guaranteed to light up the interviewer's eyes.

The problem is that you're matching the answer to the job, not to the heart. And your heart never lies when it comes to knowing what you truly want.

I love to ask questions and probe deep down into people's hearts and their dreams. When I was younger, this process used to get me in trouble.

"You're being nosy," someone once said.

"That's too personal," said others.

Now that I'm older and a bit wiser, I've come to realize that my passion for other people's passions—well, that's actually a gift. It took me a long time to learn how to use that gift in a way that gives back and helps others.

My formal education is in counseling—I have a B.S. and an M.A. tacked on the wall, but I found that traditional ways of solving problems and getting to the root of depression and misery usually compounded situations instead of changing them. In my business as a Passion Mentor, the focus is entirely on creating a life centered around joy and fulfillment, which means I help people get clear on what that looks like and they move forward with action and new habits.

Not everyone I work with is ready or willing to open up his heart and share his dreams. I've found there's a huge resistance for many people to be open about dreams, desires, hopes, and wishes because it requires us to crank up the vulnerability knob. There's a certain vulnerability that comes with sharing some of our deepest desires. Yet it is that very vulnerability that holds the keys and the clues to what we want most from life. If you are willing to be open, honest, and vulnerable about this process, that authenticity will provide you with the answers quickly.

Learning to Listen

Despite being deaf, I have a voice within me that sometimes screams pretty loud. The biggest challenge with this voice is figuring out whether it's coming from my head or my heart.

The heart knows. The heart centers the path.

The head will sway you in all kinds of directions.

I had one particular experience with an actual "voice" that truly spoke loud and clear. I was in the car on a rainy day, driving to an exhibit for my sales job. Out of the blue, I heard this voice say, "Write Keith's book."

Uh?

The voice referred to Keith St. Onge—Keith was the current World Barefoot Champion at the time, and I had taken just two barefoot water skiing lessons from him.

Yet the voice was so clear that it was as if someone were sitting in the passenger seat next to me.

I was puzzled. Did I really "hear" it, or was it just a thought that popped in my head?

Now, keep in mind, I'm deaf. Even though I can hear voices if you're talking to me, I can't understand what's being said unless I can lipread or someone is signing it.

But there I was, driving along the highway with the windshield wipers zipping back and forth, and boom, a voice tells me what to do.

That was weird.

Yet the more I thought about the message, the more I knew it was a sign to move forward with my writing path. The heart wanted to write. The heart loved barefoot water skiing. To be able to write about the very thing I was crazy passionate about—well, that was bliss, right there.

The problem was—I didn't have any experience writing a book. And I knew almost nothing about Keith. Heck, I had just met the guy. Was

I just supposed to reach out to him and say, "Hey, this voice told me to write your book"?

As crazy as the whole process was, the heart was saying, "Write. Keith's. Book."

Clear as day.

Well, there was only one surefire way to find out. I reached out to Keith, told him what had happened, and waited for a reply.

Turns out, Keith was looking for a sign, too. We partnered together for two-and-a-half years and wrote *Gliding Soles: Lessons from a Life on Water*. The journey of writing that first book was a blood, sweat, and tears experience. I learned a lot from the beginning to the end—and experience is something that is priceless.

When it comes from the heart, I know it's God's voice within me. It's a voice that's right. Every time I've chosen to ignore it, I usually trip up.

So how do you hone into this "voice" thing if you've spent your life just moseying along without guidance?

Be quiet.

Yup, that's right.

Yeah, I know the irony—this deaf writer is telling you to hush up.

Well, it's a bit more than that. If you want to skip ahead to Chapter 11: Discovering Passion Through Meditation, we'll dive deeper into this quiet stuff.

If you're busier than heck running from one thing to another (believe me, I know this "too busy to breathe" routine), you probably need to implement this quiet time state.

Now, I know it's really not fair that I can flip a switch on my hearing aids and instantly be transported into absolute silence, but to be fair, I've left my hearing aids on and worked to instill a sense of peace and quiet within—even when surrounded by a cacophony of noise.

But the quiet I'm really referring to is the process of shifting your focus to identifying the questions to which you need answers.

Go ahead; try this yourself:

Find a place where you can sit quietly, undisturbed. What are the pressing questions to which you want answers?

Now, once you've written out those questions (and come on, don't hold back—this stuff is for *you*), take the time throughout each day to be aware of the answers.

You'll receive guidance in the form of signs—perhaps a person will cross paths with you to help you out, perhaps your mood and energy will shift, maybe you'll learn something new, or a physical symbol of some kind will show up.

> *"The only way to do great work is to love what you do. If you haven't found it yet, keep looking. Don't settle. As with all matters of the heart, you'll know it when you find it."*
> ~ Steve Jobs

Beth and Ruth: Trust Your Journey

Beth Brownlee never questioned her passion while growing up. She was deep into playing sports and wanted to make a career in the sports field. Teaching and coaching seemed like the natural outlet, so Beth did that for three years after college. Very quickly, she discovered she did not like her job's politics, so she went to work at various sports companies until she arrived at Columbia sports. Her friend, Ruth Nichols, joined her at the company and the two of them enjoyed their jobs.

Personally and professionally, everything was humming along well. Then, out of the blue (that's usually how it happens, isn't it?), Beth was diagnosed with cancer.

"Chemotherapy was awful," Beth said. "I was so sick and depressed."

Friends from all over sent gifts, but one gift helped Beth tremendously. It was a gift with the words, "Trust your journey."

"For whatever reason, those three words just stopped the depression," Beth said. "I wasn't immediately well—I was still sick—but that moment, I understood that cancer is part of my journey, but not my complete journey."

During that time, Ruth's husband died and she was left to raise a toddler, alone. Beth shared the same words with Ruth, "Trust your journey." The words became a comforting symbol of support between the two of them. They started sharing the words with other women who were facing difficult times and began to notice a ripple effect—the words were helping others to get through tough times.

Beth and Ruth began listening to their intuition, which was pointing them in the direction of helping others to trust their journeys as well. They took a leave from Columbia to create a company centered around the three words.

"Passion—that's your heart's desire," Beth explained. "Not enough people follow their hearts or their intuitions. Trust the first thing you feel. That second or third voice in your head that puts doubt there, ignore that. Go with your first gut feeling and follow that. Don't allow the other voices in your head to talk you out of it."

> "The strongest guide in the process of unwrapping your passion is going to be intuition. You can interpret this in a variety of ways and call it whatever you want. We all have it within us—that little 'voice' or 'gut feeling' that gives us information. For me, it's the voice of God guiding me."
> ~ Beth Brownlee, *Trust Your Journey*

Beth and Ruth left their jobs to start their own business, Trust Your Journey, helping and inspiring others to trust their journeys. They love making a difference for others, especially for women who are facing challenging situations and need assistance breaking through to their hearts and finding their passions.

"Since the cancer journey, I handle things much differently now," Beth said. "I listen to my heart; I think it's God's voice for me. That's the voice I follow, and it brings me answers as well. I'm more open now; I don't force anything—I don't push or pull. I allow life to happen and I go with the flow."

CHAPTER 6

Putting Life Off
for Someday

"To live is the rarest thing in the
world. Most people exist, that is all."
~ Oscar Wilde

always had the thought that "someday" I would start writing a book. For years and years, however, something always stood in my way. The self-talk going on in my head was spinning out a million and one reasons why I had to put it off:

- I need more experience.
- I've never written a book.
- I don't know where to start.
- Who am I to write a book?
- I'm a nobody. Who's going to buy my book?
- My job takes up too much time. There's a thousand things I have to do to stay on top of my work.
- I just want to relax and watch a movie. I can start the book later.
- I have my hands full with three kids. When the kids are grown and gone, I'll start my book then. I'll have all the time in the world to write when I don't have all these things going on in my life.

The excuses and negative self-talk were never-ending. They provided me with all kinds of "someday" options. I was trading the time I had now for a later time.

The problem with waiting for someday is that without a plan, a timeline, a goal, and action, you'll wake up five years later with....

Nothing.

Everything changed one weekend. I was deep into reading Dan Miller's books *48 Days to the Work You Love* and *No More Dreaded Mondays* while on a seven-hour train ride to a speaking engagement. I was underlining one bit of wisdom after another when I came across this paragraph:

As Frederick Buechner said, "The place God calls you to is the place where your deep gladness and the world's deep hunger meet." Ask yourself: What is the world hungering for right now? How can I use my unique skills and talents to satisfy that hunger? Don't rest until you find your own answer.

I put the book down and dove deep into thought. I thought some more. Then all of a sudden, bits and pieces of answers began coming to me. I grabbed a notebook and started to jot down everything that was flooding in. I filled up a couple of pages with my thoughts. I wrote down my skills—everything I was "good" at. I wrote down what stirred me—all the things in life that I really enjoyed doing. A recurring theme began to show up as I continued to answer Dan's questions.

- I wanted to write.
- I wanted to tell stories about the people I met on the road of life.
- I wanted to teach.
- I wanted to speak and inspire others.
- I wanted to share my gifts.
- I wanted to help other people and make an impact in their lives.
- I wanted to leave a big, passionate mark on the world by doing all of these things, including barefoot water skiing.

Not "someday."

Now.

So right then and there, I closed Dan's book and began to write. I wrote on the train ride down and the train ride back home. I continued to write when I arrived home. I ended up self-publishing my first book—just in time for my first Coaching with Excellence workshop with Dan. I published five more books after that monumental weekend.

During an interview with Dan, he shared this message: "Take action. Too many people wait and they tell me, 'I'm not living full out; I'm not doing what I want.' They wait, and too much time passes by. Take action. Give yourself exposure to new ideas and new people. Procrastination is the friend of failure—many people are losing by living under their potential."

Dan was fortunate to have Zig Ziglar as one of his mentors. Zig taught him one of his greatest lessons, that success is not "taking" from other people, but the more you give, the more success shows up unexpectedly.

During the same interview, Dan gave me a nugget of wisdom when it comes to understanding what you love to do: "Look inward, first. We look around instead of looking inward—and how we have the confidence to do what's the perfect fit for us is to look inward first. We have to be willing to find our own authentic path."

> *"Passion gives us direction and pulls us forth in life. Passion is within us—it's definitely innate. It's the outside things—kids, family, experiences, activities—those trigger the passion within. Passion is an inside job."*
> ~ **Jason S. Moore,** *Awaken Hero Academy and Adventures*

Waiting for Perfection

Another thing I learned from Dan—whatever you do does not have to be perfect. Dan's first book, *48 Days to the Work You Love*, was actually sold in a three-ring binder at first. Perfection causes delays and procrastination. You will never deliver if you wait for perfection. The most important thing is to TAKE ACTION. That's right. ACTION. Which means you have to stop putting off your gifts, talents, skills, and dreams until "someday."

When you're aligned with your passion and purpose, there is a feeling of harmony in your life. You're doing what you were born to do. Now, this doesn't mean you won't struggle. This doesn't mean you won't encounter challenges and frustrations. Instead, when challenges and frustrations occur, you will recognize them as tolls on the journey, all of which make you stronger.

All too often, I find that the quest for perfection often gets in the way of enjoying life. People are waiting for all the ducks to be lined up, the "i" to be dotted and the "t" to be crossed, and the perfect time to arrive—before they start living the life they really want.

When I decided to take up barefoot water skiing after a twenty-plus-year absence, I was quite overweight and very out of shape. I wanted to put it off and get in shape before heading down to Florida.

I'm glad I didn't. I would still be waiting today if I waited for everything to be perfect before getting back on the water.

Because, you see, I'm still carrying extra pounds and lumpy in all the wrong places, but I now have several years of passionate living under my belt.

Perfection is the killer of dreams. Waiting for everything or anything to be perfect means that the world never gets to see your gifts. People never get to see the beautiful, imperfectly perfect human being whom you are.

I left a mistake in one of my books after publishing it. I could have easily taken it down and fixed the typo.

But I left it in there.

I often give this book as a gift or hand it out at workshops. It's a simple writing journal with inspirational quotes about passion. The book is a reminder to keep our focus on our joy—to do things in life that matter and to live with gratitude.

The typo I left in there is a wonderful reminder to celebrate life in all it's glorious imperfections.

(And hey, if you saw that punctuation mistake, it is okay, I put it there as a lesson. Let it go.)

So that thing you're putting off until everything is perfect....

Quit waiting.

Hey, Baby, Your Time Is Running Out!

From the moment we're born, the proverbial stopwatch has been set. Time starts ticking the minute we take our first breath.

With each passing day that we're alive, it's easy to become more and more complacent to the idea that our lives stretch out before us. "I have time," we say.

We gamble the time we have now, with the idea that we'll have plenty of time later to do the things we really want to do.

I see this a lot in people who are biding their time until retirement. Retirement is the "someday" they're banking on.

The one thing people work so darned hard for over many, many years is this:

Freedom to do what they want with their time.

The problem with working for the sake of just getting through life to "retirement" is that without passion, purpose, and something greater, time freedom becomes an empty entity.

So let me tell you about my friend, sixty-four-year-old John Berry. John and I connected through Facebook. We both shared a passion for barefoot water skiing. John was one of the early skiers—he picked up the sport back in 1968, when very few people could glide on their feet. At age fifty-seven, John learned to barefoot water ski backwards—something he initially thought he was too old to try. John and I met up to barefoot together during a recent trip to Florida. It was easy to see that John was very passionate about everything in life. His energy was bright, vibrant, and engaging. He and his wife, Patti, were definitely enjoying retirement.

John worked for a phone company in Ohio for thirty-three years. He didn't plan a career in the telecommunications industry. Right after high school graduation, John's father sat him down and said, "John, you don't have much ambition; you better go get a job with a public utility." John applied to every utility in the area; the phone company was the first one to call him back and hire him.

John fell in love with the job.

"I loved fixing people's problems—people were always happy to see me," John said. "I loved the outdoor work, loved the guys I worked with—six of us raised families together, played baseball and went bowling together. I just got lucky—I was blessed. I never had any thoughts of leaving or changing jobs."

The day he retired from his job, John went to work a half hour early to make coffee for everyone, something he had done for years.

John then realized that the one thing that brought him joy was to be able to serve others. So he went to work again, this time for a social services agency. He told me:

> I work with many different kinds of people who have many different kinds of problems—homelessness, drug addictions, and those who have just left the criminal justice system. I've found that I love serving people and working with people.
>
> I love serving God, as well. Most of my life I didn't even realize how full of grace and blessed I was.

John and Patti both serve by teaching Sunday school at their church, and John has served missions in Haiti. Every Tuesday, John takes Patti on an adventure for the day. Every week, it's a surprise as to where they are going and what they will do.

John tells me he has a great day, every day, despite some of the struggles he's been through in his life. I asked John what was the secret to his high level of energy, passion, and joy--and how he was able to sustain it all these years. He replied:

You have to look in the mirror every day—and you have to be honest with that person in the mirror. You have to love yourself. Be truthful and confident in yourself. Go find a person to share yourself with and share your attitude with. People today are greedy; they want to hold it in and not share. The secret is to let go and help other people. Serve other people. Be generous to others. All of that will come back to you—the more you pay it forward, the more that comes back to you.

"I define passion in two different ways; one way, it's a feeling of love, warmth, and comfort. I also define it as desire, something you want to do, something you want to learn, or something you want to experience—and you have to put in a great deal of effort to get there. It's difficult to obtain great rewards unless you put in great effort or make great sacrifices—you don't get that sitting on the couch at home— then the rewards are phenomenal. When you have a passion for something and you love it, the rewards are great—and the rewards are available to everyone."
~ **John Berry**

So there are two lessons here: one, don't keep putting off life for retirement and two, keep passion and purpose alive in your retirement years. Or better yet, never "retire." Live with passion until your last day!

The Decision-Making Process

In one of her columns of "What I Know for Sure," Oprah Winfrey wrote, "When you suppress your authentic self and postpone your joy and deny your passion—a part of you dies. You don't notice it, because you're going through the routines of daily life."

It's all too easy to let life creep up on you. There's a simple question that I use as a tool for determining what really matters in life:

If you were lying on your deathbed in six months, what would you look back on with regret?

Ask yourself this: How would you feel if your time was suddenly limited and you could never complete the work, book, or project you really want to do? Because really, your time *is* limited. From the day we're born, the countdown to dying begins. You're gambling that you'll have forever if you continue in the comfort of what you're feeling now.

With every decision you're stuck on, here's a simple process you can use to cut through the muck and arrive at a clear decision:

Imagine yourself six months, one year, or five years into the future and look back on the decision you're about to make.

- What will you gain or lose from your decision today?
- What is the end result of this decision if you don't pursue it?
- What is the end result of this decision if you do pursue it?
- What will you rejoice about with your decision?
- What will you regret with your decision?
- Does this decision move you closer or further from your dreams and passions?

To make the process even simpler, the one rule for passion is this: Do it *now*. Not later. Not someday.

> *"What do you dream of doing with your life? Do it. Begin right now and never quit. There is greatness in you. Let it out. Be persistent."*
> ~ Bob Proctor

My friend, Doreen Coady, and her husband, Mike, know all too well how life can turn around in an instant. Their nineteen-year-old son, Michael, slipped on an icy edge while snowboarding and went tumbling down. Doreen wasn't too concerned when she received the call to come to the hospital. She and Mike contemplated whether or not to grab a quick breakfast, but they decided to head straight to the hospital.

Michael's friends looked pale and green when they walked in. Doreen ended up reassuring them. "Don't worry; he will be fine."

Doreen was still in denial when she saw Michael with a head-stabilizing brace. In fact, she asked the doctor whether he would still be able to go on an upcoming trip to Brazil.

The doctor knew Michael had sustained permanent damage to his spinal cord, but he didn't have the courage to explain the extent of his paralysis.

But Mike understood the impact of the damage. Once outside of the room, he slid down the wall, crying.

"If you have anything you want to do in life, you should hurry up and do it," Michael told them. "Don't put anything off. This could happen to you."

So while Michael was recovering, his parents sat down to make a Dream List. "Our son's advice was serious," Doreen said. "We asked each other about our dreams and goals and wrote them down."

They dove into their list:

- Swim with the dolphins.
- Go to the Magic Kingdom.
- Get several tattoos.
- See Tony Robbins.
- Renew our vows in Vegas.
- Go to an Iron Maiden concert.
- Open a custom motorcycle shop.

So they did it all.

"Through it all, we came to realize the importance of having and living your dreams," Doreen explained. "Passion is whatever your heart tells you. At any minute, our lives can change. Before my son's injury, we weren't living intentionally. We thought we had forever ahead of us. We don't. So we live with joy and fulfillment squeezed into a short life."

As for Michael, from the moment he broke his neck, he knew he was paralyzed. He spent two long years in rehabilitation to try to get as much motion back as possible, but he did it with a positive attitude. He jumped right back into living a full life. Instead of looking back in sorrow, he chose to look ahead and focus on what he could do. Today, Michael is married and studying to become a lawyer.

Dying While Living

Back when I was in my second year of motherhood, I came across this little ditty in a magazine, author unknown:

First I was dying to finish high school and start college.

And then I was dying to finish college and start working.

And then I was dying to marry and have children.

And then I was dying for my children to grow old enough for school so I could return to work.

And then I was dying to retire.

And now, I am dying....

And suddenly realize I forgot to live.

For many years, I lived with these words inside of me as a reminder to enjoy the parenting journey. And for the most part, I did. But slowly, ever so slowly, the routine of life took over.

I forgot.

I was sucked up so deep into the daily routine that I forgot about myself. I forgot what sparked passion inside of me. I forgot what it was like to be joyful and hopeful.

There's a quote that's often attributed to Benjamin Franklin (the origin has never been verified) that says, "Some people die at twenty-five but aren't buried until seventy-five."

I was fortunate. I stepped back into one of the passions of my younger days, and in the process, I learned:

- You really can reinvent yourself.
- Every moment of every day has the potential for a brand new start.
- You really can improve from where you are now.
- You must choose your thoughts and actions carefully. They matter.

Why You Can't Put Off Living

A few months ago, I started watching TED Talks in the evening before going to bed. I came across Scott Dinsmore's talk, "How to Find Work You Love." He set out to find the 20 percent of people who passionately love what they do, versus the 80 percent who were living lives of quiet desperation.

To everyone he met, he asked a simple question, "Why are you doing the work you're doing?"

The answer from those in the 80 percent group was often, "Well, because somebody told me I'm supposed to."

So for the 80 percent who aren't too crazy about what they do, in many cases, they're climbing a ladder set against the wrong wall.

Scott came away with a framework of three principles for creating a life centered around passionate work:

1. Understand yourself, because if you don't know what you're looking for, you're never going to find it.
2. Decide your framework for making decisions—what really matters to you?
3. Create and learn from your experiences. Pay attention to what you're learning and apply it to your life. What experiences are important? Which ones do you want to repeat?

The key is to find the work/passion that you can't possibly *not* do. The work/passion that if your life ended tomorrow, you'd be filled with regret for not living life the way you truly wanted to.

So Scott left a high-paying job to create Live Your Legend and use his skills to help others discover the work they are meant to do, work that is fulfilling, meaningful, and passionate.

In his TED talk, Scott explains:

I don't care what it is that you're into, what passion, what hobby. If you're into knitting, you can find someone who is killing it knitting, and you can learn from them. It's wild. And that's what this whole day is about, to learn from the folks speaking, and we profile these people on Live Your Legend every day, because when ordinary people are doing the extraordinary, and we can be around that, it becomes normal. And this isn't about being Gandhi or Steve Jobs, doing something crazy. It's just about doing something that matters to you, and makes an impact that only you can make.

Just a short time after I discovered Scott's TED talk, I learned he died while climbing Mt. Kilimanjaro. A beautiful, passionate soul is no longer with us, but he indeed left a legacy for us to learn from. Here is a final nugget of wisdom from him:

I have just one question to ask you guys, and I think it's the only question that matters. And it's what is the work you can't not do? Discover that, live it, not just for you, but for everybody around you, because that is what starts to change the world. What is the work you can't *not* do?

CHAPTER 7

Getting Beyond Fear

"A lot of people think that bold people have no fear. That's not true. Boldness is not the absence of fear, but rather, the recognition that the best things are worth conquering your fear over."
~ Randy Gage

What's the number one thing that holds people back from living truly passionate lives?

Fear.

And a lot of times, you have no idea that little "F" word is lurking in your life, holding you back.

Fear is nothing more than a dark enemy that lies within us. Physically, it's like a medicine ball that weighs you down. Mentally, it's a dark cloud that permeates your thoughts and leaves you with the feeling of no escape.

My friend Craig MacFarlane is blind. Totally blind, yet he travels all over the world by himself. No guide dog. No cane. Craig skied down a mountain at 50 mph. He has gone over a water ski jump without knowing where he was going to land. He has played hockey, shooting at a goal that he cannot see. He has learned to embrace fear and plow right through it. Craig often says, "If you're not living on the edge, you're taking up too much space."

When was the last time you challenged yourself to live on the edge, to feel the excitement of something new and unknown?

When you do something that you are passionate about, you are willing to challenge yourself to do more than you ever thought you could do—you step way, way, *way* out of your comfort zone when you live on the edge.

Fear manifests itself in different ways:

- Insecurity
- Uncertainty
- Discomfort
- Anxiety
- Unease

How many times have you looked at bold, successful people and thought, "They're not afraid of anything—they have no fear!"

But the truth is, bold, successful people push right through the very same fears that hold most people back. There's a quote by Ambrose Redmoon that sums it up: "Courage is not the absence of fear, but rather the judgment that something else is more important than fear."

So it comes down to this: How bad do you want what you want? How deep is the desire? Are you willing to do whatever it takes to get where you want to go, to do what you want to do, to accomplish what you want to accomplish?

Are you willing to push through the fear to get there?

The first time I got into the boat for a barefoot water ski lesson down in Florida, I asked the World Barefoot Champion instructor a crucial question.

"Are there any alligators in this lake?"

"Yes, there are, but alligators don't come near the boat because the engine noise scares them away," the World Champion explained.

I don't think I caught anything after the word, "Yes."

Alligators in the lake!

I pictured a hungry thirteen-footer slithering through the weeds....

I quickly had to get that movie out of my head because I was about to attempt my first barefoot water ski run more than twenty years after becoming deaf from a fall while barefooting as a teen. I was going to get into the same body of water that was home to at least a handful or perhaps a couple of hundred reptiles.

(Much later, I discovered there are 600 alligators per square mile in that area.)

Passion was about to outweigh fear.

Sure enough, the moment I put my feet on the water, the years literally melted away. In one quick rush, the old passion for the sport came flooding back. I didn't give the alligators another thought that day. Now that I was hooked, I wanted more. The second time I went for a lesson, I still didn't give the lake reptiles much thought. I was too darn excited about being able to walk on top of the water again.

The third time was a different story. It was Women's Barefoot Week, and the thought of spending an entire week in the same water with leathery creatures with big teeth certainly wasn't a thrilling thought.

I didn't tell anyone about my fears at first.

That is, until the nightmares began.

Let me tell you, when an alligator comes at you in the middle of the night, it creates a heart-stopping, *oh-my-gosh-I-can't-sleep* situation. After the second night of nightmares, I shared my fears with the other gals. Admitting the fear seemed to be the logical first step in dealing with it.

But...admitting your fears and dealing with them are two different things.

"Everything you want is on the other side of fear."
~ Jack Canfield

What Price Are You Paying for Fear?

When it comes to pursuing dreams or doing new things, fear is one thing that holds many people back.

Fear of success.

Fear of failure.

Fear of mistakes.

Fear of disappointment.

Fear of what other people think.

Fear of appearing like a fool.

Fear of _____ (fill in the blank).

What fears are holding you back? Come on; let's get down and dirty here and really write out the scariest thing that could possibly happen in your life if you were to dive passionately into something you really love to do. Spill it out:

_____

_____

_____

_____

_____

_____

_____

All fear stems from the imagined and the unknown. The human mind is very powerful in dreaming up scenarios that feed on fear.

And here's the thing: You attract what you fear. How do I know this? Because alligators started showing up in my life left and right. I came face-to-face with an alligator in the road while walking down a street in Florida.

One of my barefoot coaches told me I needed to face my fears by getting up close and touching an alligator. "You need to see them for the magnificent creatures they are."

I broke out in a cold sweat at the very thought. "Are you crazy?" I said. "I'm so scared now, what makes you think I can even get up close with one?"

Facing Your Fears Head On

"Most fear and doubt arises out of ignorance and feelings of inadequacy," Brian Tracy writes in his book *Goals· How to Get Everything You Want Faster Than You Thought Possible.* "The more you learn what you need to know to achieve your goals, the less fear you will feel on the one hand and the more courage and confidence you will feel on the other." So you know what that means—the only way around fear is right through it. Right smack-dab *through* it. As Jack Canfield says, "Everything you want is on the other side of fear." The biggest challenge is often taking that first step and moving through the fear. When you get to that other side, you've gained an experience that changes you forever.

In a twist of irony, a friend introduced me to Ken Cowles, a fellow barefoot water skier who was a gator trapper for Florida. At the time, I was seeking help in dealing with my fears because they seemed to be escalating whenever I went to Florida to ski. I was also experiencing more frequent nightmares at home. I decided it was time to learn more about alligators and find ways I could either deal with or diminish the fear.

I was really curious about Ken's story. Why would anyone want to face those beasts on a regular basis?

It's definitely not for the money, because capturing alligators is a tough, dangerous job that requires a lot of time and financial resources to make it happen.

When I first contacted Ken, I jokingly (actually, I was serious) asked him to get rid of the gators from the lakes I ski on every year in Florida. He laughed. Apparently, he's used to those kinds of requests. Ken's own foray into the alligator business came about after he called a trapper to remove some large alligators from a lake he and his kids were skiing on. Ken was so fascinated with the process that he began to learn the skills involved in catching gators.

A passion was born, and so was a job.

Alligators are known to be lightning fast and extremely powerful. During one call, Ken arrived to find a gator on a sidewalk outside of a home. When he approached, the gator turned and ran. Ken chased after it, running at full speed, but he still couldn't catch up with it. "I was running as fast as I could and it was pulling away," Ken recalled. "I threw my lariat and, by luck, noosed it like a cowboy at a rodeo."

Ken has removed alligators from an eight-foot fence (yes, they can climb!) and a second floor condominium. He has climbed into storm drain pipes and hauled them out of there. He's removed them after they've killed swimmers.

No wonder I was fearful of those pre-historic beasts!

So Ken began to introduce the idea of getting up close with an alligator. "We need to conquer that fear you harbor," he said.

I thought about it—he was right. That day, our plans for barefoot water skiing fell through, and he invited me into the backyard to "play with a gator."

I knew that if I chickened out, there was *no way* I could ever tell other people to face their fears when it comes to doing what they really love to do. I would be a hypocrite every time I coached, spoke, or wrote about fear associated with passion.

I trusted Ken. I knew he would keep me safe. Yet the minute he hauled that ten-foot gator out of the trailer and placed him on the ground, I began to shake. The gator's huge tail rocked back and forth. The gator clearly was not happy. And neither was I.

Holy freaking moly. The fear.

There was no way I could do it.

Whose stupid idea was this? I could have just stayed home. Why did I agree to this?

Ken starting talking in a calm, soothing manner. He motioned for me to come closer. I swear, he must have hypnotized me in some way because I started to inch closer and closer in baby steps.

I just wanted to get it over with.

First, he had me touch the gator's throat. To my utter surprise, the skin was soft. He motioned for me to come around and sit on the gator. It was a now or never moment. I closed my eyes and sat on the alligator. I was hysterical inside. Ken sat behind me and held the gator's head so it wouldn't move.

But the rest of the gator did.

I was done. I jumped off.

Yet I had done it! I had sat on a freaking alligator!

It took a few hours to stop shaking inside.

Looking back, that is what I define as an "Awe" moment, or more of a "Holy Crap, I Did That!" moment. We need more moments like that in our lives. There's a part of you that comes alive when you do something you think you cannot do and you get to the other side of it.

It might surprise you to know that my fear of alligators is still present, despite facing my fears over and over each time I slip into the water to take a barefooting run down in Florida. My coaches and fellow barefooters are well aware of those fears, so I've taken some good-natured ribbing along the way. A recent Christmas present from a fellow skier was a stuffed alligator. Another bought a T-shirt with an alligator on it. One friend sent me an alligator purse.

As I look back on the last several years, the lesson of fear has played out in various areas of my life time and time again. The fear of the unknown. The fear of trying something new. The fear of failing over and over again. The fear of looking like a fool in front of people. I know if I had given into the fears, I would have let a lot of dreams fall to the wayside. I would have never known the passion that comes from the other side. I would have never known that I could barefoot water ski backwards on one foot at the age of forty-eight.

If you continually play safe and do everything you can to avoid fear, one of two things will happen:

- Your life will flat-line. It will become predictable and routine.
- Your life will become predictable and routine. It will flat-line.

Either way, the outcome is the same. The problem with playing it completely safe and avoiding fear at all costs is that you never reach the edge of what you can do or feel. The price of playing it safe: regret.

Every time you face a new fear, a new apprehension, or a new challenge, ask yourself what's on the other side of that. Chances are, on the other side you'll find growth, passion, and joy.

Isn't it worth it?

CHAPTER 8

Bringing in Mentors

"Without personal growth, you can
never reach your potential."
~ John Maxwell

W ay back when I was in elementary school, there was a poster on the wall with a turkey on it. The caption said: "You can't soar like an eagle if you're surrounded by turkeys." I wish I had paid more attention to that poster and applied it to my life more. It took me a long time to recognize people in my life who were sucking the energy out of me and weighing me down. You must be strong enough to say "No" to giving your time to people who drain you.

Jim Rohn says, "You are the average of the five people you spend the most time with." Look carefully at the people you're surrounding yourself with. Are they bringing you up, pushing you to new heights, and taking you out of your comfort zone? Or are they pulling you down and sucking the life out of you on a path of mediocrity?

Check your energy levels—what energy are you putting out to the world? Does your energy light up other people's lives or dim them?

By the same token, you absorb energy from others. That's why it's so important to surround yourself with people who are highly passionate and energetic about life. Energy is contagious. What you emit is absorbed, and vice versa.

The world would have happier people if they were living their passions.

I met Tom Ziglar and Howard Partridge at a business expo in Chicago. Tom is the son of Zig Ziglar, "America's most influential and beloved encourager," whose book, *See You at the Top* has sold over two million copies. Both Tom and Howard are international business coaches and they have trained hundreds of thousands of business and salespeople worldwide. Their energy and passion for what they do is amazing and continues year after year. I had the opportunity to interview both of them for this book, and I loved the lessons they shared, so I'm featuring both of them in separate stories.

Tom Ziglar

Tom started working for the Ziglar Corporation right out of college. His heart wasn't quite into his work for he had another dream: he wanted to become a professional golfer. For two years, he passionately pursued the sport, working hard to improve his game. Then two things happened around the same time; he suffered an injury, and he moved into sales at work.

"I started to realize my golf career was inhibited by my lack of talent," Tom said. "I loved sales—my passion for sales took almost two years to develop after I started working there."

Tom remembers the night he realized his passion for his work. His father was scheduled to be a surprise speaker at an event for over thirty thousand people. Tom was setting up the product tables and covering the books.

"Is Zig Ziglar speaking tonight?" a man asked.

"Well, don't tell," Tom admitted, smiling at him.

"Will he be signing autographs here? I'm going to stand in line now."

Tom tried to convince him to come back later since it would be hours before Zig could sign books, but the man stood firm. He wanted to meet with Zig.

"Tell me your story," Tom said.

The man was from Central America, but he had moved to Chicago to live with his brother. After three weeks, he quickly realized he needed to master English to be able to find a job and make a living. His brother gave him a copy of Zig's book, *See You at the Top*.

"The book changed my life," he told Tom, through his tears. "I was an alcoholic, my wife was going to leave me. Because of your dad, my life has changed. So standing here, waiting, is an honor."

That was the moment when Tom connected his work with passion. "That's when I really connected my career at Ziglar with what we do," Tom said. "When hope is born, how it gives people inspiration and when people's lives change—that's how I fell in love with what I do. I just want to help change people's lives."

Tom became president of Ziglar Corporation at the tender age of thirty. Just three years later, he faced a situation that would challenge him to the core: he launched a business idea that put the company two-and-half-million dollars into debt.

"The business was fantastic the first thirty days, then the next thirty was okay, then after that, we were bleeding money," Tom said. "My dad had his reputation on the line, and with one decision, I almost destroyed it. That was a hard thing to accept and to try to overcome."

So Tom sought the advice of the best person possible: his dad. True to Ziglar form, Zig took his son through the problem-solving process:

1. First, try to understand what put you in the negative situation in the first place. Stop digging the hole that got you in there.

2. Set up a step-by-step process on how to get out of it. Little decisions will add up every day.

3. Tell everyone the truth about what you're going through. Communicate. Talk to your team, your business partners, and customers. Let them know you're experiencing a challenge and that you're working through it.

4. Do everything you can during the day to work hard, to do your best, and then at the end of the day, put it aside and spend time with your family.

5. Feed your mind with positive, inspirational information.

"I was fortunate to spend time with my dad, the most inspirational person on earth," Tom said. "He told me, 'There's nothing to worry about; we did the best we could. God is going to handle it. We all make decisions that we learn from—some are more expensive than others, and don't do it again.' The simple or most direct way is the best way to address challenges."

Tom believes our passion and purpose are linked. One of the clues to our passion and our purpose is to pay attention to what other people come to you for—what problems do people ask you to solve? "Passion is the ultimate desire; it is the things that make you become alive. God gives us passion; it makes sense to pursue what God put in us," Tom said.

> "Did you know that every human being is created with a purpose and that they have a responsibility to not only discover their purpose but also to fulfill it?
> ~ Tom and Zig Ziglar, *Born to Win*

Howard Partridge

When Howard Partridge was eighteen years old, his stepfather kicked him out of the house after the two of them got into a fight. Howard headed west to Houston with just twenty-five cents in his pocket and eventually snagged a job as a waiter. Shortly after getting married, Howard took the wedding money and opened his first business from the trunk of his car. Since then, Howard has developed turn-key business systems, and he is passionate about helping others create phenomenal lifestyles and businesses that make an impact.

"Passion is the result of purpose," Howard explained. "The reason people are passionate is because they care about something—they have a 'why.' Unfortunately, there are a lot of people who don't have passion, and they don't think they have a purpose. They can't see how their lives matter, and they don't realize the relationship between their own actions and the outcomes."

There are two kinds of passion, Self-Centered and Other-Centered, Howard explained. Self-Centered passion is negative and selfish—it comes out when people feel they are wronged or when they have a sense of entitlement. Other-Centered passion is remarkable and extraordinary—it's about making a difference in the world for someone else.

I asked Howard, "How do you recognize passion in your own life?"

"I think your passion comes from your calling, and until we understand who we are called to be, you won't have passion," Howard said. "Everyone has a gift, and when you discover your gift and your calling, then your passion comes alive. I didn't discover mine until recent years. I'm in the coaching business. When I look back on my life, even when I was a kid, I could always notice how something could be better— the person, the situation, the room—I noticed how to improve things. I didn't utilize that gift at the time. Sometimes it takes a challenging situation to bring out the best in us; that's how it happened for me."

For someone who says, "I have no passion for anything," Howard disagrees. Passion is within us, but we intentionally have to choose to create a life that matters. Howard takes part in John Maxwell's mastermind group. One of the ways John Maxwell teaches to dial into your passion is to ask a series of questions:

- What do you cry about?
- What do you sing about?
- What do you dream about?

"If you truly care about other people, I think that's where you have to start," Howard said. "Do you want to make a difference in the world?

You can be passionate about a hobby, or saving money, or something nice for yourself, but the type of positive passion I'm talking about is about making a difference in the world for someone else. Start by thinking about what you cry about, what are the injustices of life you want to solve.

"Never let anyone stop you from doing what you're called to do."

Watch Out for Energy Vampires

Judith Orloff has a term for the people who suck the life out of you: Energy Vampires. In her book *Positive Energy*, Judith cautions us to watch out for people who drain our energy. They can be literally anyone we live with or cross paths with. All too often, we allow ourselves to be sucked into an Energy Vampire's drama without even realizing we're spiraling down with the person.

The biggest cost of spending time with someone who sucks the life out of you is that you give away precious time from your own life.

> *"You breathe in the energy of people around you."*
> ~ James Atlucher

Years ago, I became friends with another mom, and we often spent time together while our kids played. I found myself exhausted, but I chalked it up to the fact that I was a mom with three little kids.

One night, we had dinner together while our husbands watched the kids. I was excited when I arrived and totally looking forward to a rare night out without a little one clinging to me.

As the dinner went on, I found the energy slowly draining from me as this mom went on and on about various topics, all with a negative slant. I tried to steer toward a more positive conversation, but it was short-lived.

On the way home, I decided I would no longer hang out with this mom. As difficult as it was to put a stop to our gatherings, it was for the better. I chose to interact and share time with other mothers whose energy and perspectives fueled me, instead.

It can be extremely challenging to be around Energy Vampires who are family members or coworkers whom you see on a regular basis. The key is to set up boundaries or continually take breaks from draining situations.

Kevin Hall: The Importance of Mentors

As is probably obvious by now, one of my favorite life-changing books is *Aspire* by Kevin Hall. Kevin was the second of two boys born to an alcoholic father and raised by a single mom (who was a teen at the time). His mother was a recovered alcoholic who became a substance abuse counselor. She guided him with powerful words, "You can do anything that you want in life. You can achieve and live every worthwhile dream."

A Jesuit priest taught Kevin that we are spiritual beings having a human experience. "I believe we can do anything using our capacity and potential if it fits within our God-given gifts," Kevin said. "When you go after something, the universe conspires to make it happen. When you make a decision, it becomes an action. There's nothing we can't go out and do—it's up to us."

Kevin has tested himself by biking in the Leadville 100, a grueling mountain bike race that takes place annually in Colorado.

When I asked him how he overcame his fears in life, he told me:

People who are stuck in routine are not dreaming. They are probably functioning from fear versus love. Fear says, "I am not enough." It creates a scarcity mentality. If you believe you are not enough, you won't be able to achieve it. I've always quoted Joseph Campbell: "The cave we fear to enter has the treasure we seek." Successful people fear, but they go into the cave—the fear decreases. The cave we fear to enter holds the treasure—when you love yourself.

When I coach someone, I work on the inside—how you feel about yourself. Practice Genshai—a Hindi word that means never to believe in yourself as "small."

Go after bigger things. Use affirmations: "I am worthy. I'm capable. I trust myself."

When you live in the opposite, "I don't have a gift, I'm mad at the world, I'm not going to forgive," then you're living in the past. You have one foot on the gas, and the other one on the brake. Let go of the brake, let go of the past, of the victim in you.

Your purpose is not about you; it's your gift to the world. Figure out who needs your purpose, who needs your leadership, who needs your gifts. Shift from fear and, instead, function out of love.

Remember, whenever you are on a passionate path in life, you will meet others on your path who share the same level of passion or more. Kevin introduced me to Susanne Lammot, a seventy-three-year-old pediatrician (still practicing because she's passionate about her patients!) who became my roommate at a Genshai retreat. Susanne and her sister, Martha, grew up sailing on oceans.

Martha's passion is skiing—she was a ski instructor for thirty-one years in Aspen. Susanne's son created a career on the water, capturing a bronze in the Olympics, winning the U.S. Team Racing Nationals three times, and sailing with the New Zealand team in America's Cup. A passionate family, indeed.

A few days after the retreat, Susanne asked me to call her. "I know this is crazy and we just met, but I won a Nu Skin trip to Maui and I'd like to invite you on the trip. My sister is going as well."

The three of us had a wonderful time on that trip seeing whales and going snorkeling. In another amazing case of synchronicity, during one of the presentations, a familiar face popped up in a video. It was my youngest son's pediatrician, who left behind his career to join the company full time. The two of us met up on yet another trip during one of my speaking gigs.

One of the wonderful things that happens when you connect with your passions is that you will surround yourself with people who nurture your passionate energy so it will reach even higher levels.

Stay aware of those who are the Energy Vampires in your life, and choose to give your time and energy to those who uplift and raise you higher, rather than bringing you down and sucking the energy out of you.

CHAPTER 9

Having Passionate Fun

> *"If you're not having fun, you
> haven't discovered your 'why.'"*
> ~ Terry Hadaway

All work and no play makes Jack a dull boy.

When I was growing up, the concept of work was all about money and security. Work was the safe, steady job that you obtained after high school or college. Pretty much everyone on my suburban block did the same thing—they went to work, came home, watched some TV, and then repeated it all over again the next day. Weekends were reserved for yard work, house repairs, and some more TV. There was the occasional vacation. The dream stuff was reserved for people who were way outside the box.

You've probably heard the story about a group of blind tourists who were invited to feel an elephant for the first time.

"It's long and skinny," said the one feeling the tail.

"Actually, it feels like a snake," said the one feeling the trunk.

"It is built like a cylinder," said the one feeling the elephant's leg.

"This thing is huge!" said the one feeling the belly. "I can't even feel the top of it!"

The point of this story shows how limited our thoughts and beliefs can be if we aren't exposed to a world that's bigger than what we're currently experiencing.

You want a bigger, more passionate life? Learn from others who are further along the path and going in the direction you want to go.

> *"Tell me, what do you plan to do with your one wild and precious life?"*
> ~ Mary Oliver

One of my passions is to "have fun with everything I do." It's the same thing that Jack Canfield wrote when he took the Passion Test given by Janet Attwood, the author of *The Passion Test.*

Why is this so important—having fun?

When you're having fun, you're experiencing joy.

Stress kills passion. When you are stressed, you suppress the part of the brain that expresses emotions. The antidote to stress is to do the things that bring you joy. To play, to dream, to wonder, and to wander. You actually have to schedule time to play—or better yet, choose work that is your play.

Becoming deaf could have easily been the worst thing that ever happened to me. And at the time, that's exactly what I thought—that being deaf was a truly awful thing. I struggled for months. A simple change of attitude, however, turned everything around for me.

Now don't get me wrong—there are times I'll still throw a pity party here and there when I feel cut off from people due to lack of communication access or when encountering negative attitudes from others.

Most of the time, it takes a simple reminder from a friend to get back on track and to keep the focus in a positive direction. A simple shift in my thoughts, attitude, or actions are all that's often needed to bring in joy once again.

The same shift will happen to you when you focus on passion and bringing it into your life.

If you focus on the million and one reasons why you can't—that's exactly what you'll end up with—barriers to your passions and joy.

Now, I'd like to challenge you to create a life where your work and your fun are entwined. A quote by François-René de Chateaubriand, a nineteenth-century French writer and diplomat, sums up this idea perfectly:

> A master in the art of living draws no sharp distinction between his work and his play; his labor and his leisure; his mind and his body; his education and his recreation. He hardly knows which is which. He simply pursues his vision of excellence through whatever he is doing, and leaves others to determine whether he is working or playing. To himself, he always appears to be doing both.

Rick Griffin and Sandi McKenna: Internet Friends Become Travel Partners

I "met" Rick Griffin and Sandi McKenna on Twitter a couple of years back when they created the Midlife Road Trip Tour. In fact, they "met" on Twitter. They're a wonderful example of making work your play and vice versa. When it comes to travel, these two are experts, but they certainly didn't start out that way.

Rick's desire for something more in life came when he was lying in a hospital bed battling an acute infection of pancreatitis. He didn't know whether he would live or die.

"I was lying there thinking, 'I'm too young to die, I haven't seen the Grand Canyon,'" Rick recalled.

So many things were on his bucket list. As soon as he recovered, Rick decided to rearrange his priorities to pursue the things he really wanted to do. He sold his daycare business and took his family to see the Grand Canyon.

"I don't want to get to the end of my life and look back and say, 'I wish I did.' That's one of the things I thought about when I was laying there in the hospital."

Back home, Rick channeled his creativity into a new business and opened a video production company, producing commercials for banks, hospitals, churches, and local businesses.

When business was slow, Rick went on the web in search of contests. He started winning a few here and there. That's how he discovered Twitter and began to put out regular tweets.

Sandi lived in Tampa and produced TV segments. The two of them began to chat on Twitter, exchanging some of their wishes and dreams. Travel was one that pulled them in the same direction.

At this same time, Sandi's father was in the last year of his life, battling an illness, so Sandi was feeling the tug to do something meaningful with her own life.

The idea of doing a Midlife Road Tour started very casually and grew very organically. Rick and Sandi met in Tampa and hit it off instantly. They discovered they shared the same values: family, trust, faith, and honesty. They both shared a passion for making people laugh, creative work, and producing great stories for visual media.

So they created a website, started sharing their bucket lists, and planned their trips around each item. Before long, they had an online community that gave them suggestions, travel tips, and bucket list items. Rick was the adventurous, daredevil one, but they both had a fear of heights. Rick's biggest dream was skydiving. Sandi's was riding a mule down a steep cliff.

"Sometimes the things that make you the most uncomfortable are the most memorable," Sandi said.

"People are content to accept mediocrity," Rick said. "I did that for many years—put off doing what I want to do. Life is more exciting out of the comfort zone. Every day is a little different and brings something new."

Sponsors began to take notice of their travels and offered to fund their trips.

"Money wasn't important, but, of course, you have to have money to survive," Rick said. "The happiness comes from doing something you love and are passionate about—that is worth something. I don't earn as much money as when I ran my business; following your passion is the reward itself. It took time before Sandi and I could do this full time, but now we can. If you follow your passion, the reward will come. Find others with the same passion—you can share the passion and the money will follow."

"*Passion means dreaming big, following your heart, going after it—not letting up, not giving up, not letting disappointment beat you or stop you from doing what you love and finding fulfillment—that's what passion means to me.*"

~ Sandi McKenna

CHAPTER 10

Identifying Your Passion Barometers

"Passion is energy. Feel the power that comes from focusing on what excites you."
~ Oprah Winfrey

The barometer of passion is to pay attention to your energy levels. What energy are you putting out to the world? Remember that question from earlier: does your energy light up other people's lives or does it dim them? When you are deep into something you enjoy doing, time passes quickly. You literally lose all sense of the passage of time. This is because your mind is deeply and fully engaged in what you're doing.

When you are living with passion, there is a heightened energy that comes with doing what makes your heart come alive.

I'm often pretty keyed up and excited at the anticipation of engaging in anything I truly love to do. There's a feeling of "Holy cow, I *get* to do this!" that accompanies passion.

When I started a speaking business, people often left comments on my Facebook wall that it seemed like I was never home—that I was always going somewhere and having fun. They didn't realize that people were paying me to do what I love to do!

And here's a cool thought: When you do what you love to do, you can't imagine retiring!

The most passionate people often can't explain the "why" of what they do, but they can explain the joy, the fired-up feeling, the "grip" of passion on their souls. Passion is the fuel that will keep you going when the going gets tough.

> *"Passion will push you above and beyond."*
> ~ **Keith St. Onge**, 2X *World Barefoot Champion*

Right now as I'm writing this, I'm nursing a sore neck from a rough fall while barefoot water skiing backward. At 39 mph, the impact sometimes feels like hitting concrete. At times, the sport can be brutal, and it has a long learning curve.

So why do I do it? What keeps me going?

All I know is that when I put my feet on the water, I come alive. And when I learn a new trick or a new skill, there's a "holy freaking moly" moment of accomplishing something that's lined right up with my passion.

Joseph Campbell believed that our passion barometer lies in our happiest moments. "The way to find out about your happiness is to keep your mind on those moments when you feel most happy, when you really are happy—not excited, not just thrilled, but deeply happy. What is it that makes you happy? Stay with it no matter what people tell you. This is what I call following your bliss."

> *"The heart of human excellence often begins to beat when you discover a pursuit that absorbs you, frees you, challenges you, or gives you a sense of meaning, joy, or passion."*
> ~ Terry Orlick

Nichole Kelly: The "Hell Yes" Barometer

What would you do differently if you knew you could lose your mind in an instant?

That was the situation Social Media Explorer CEO Nichole Kelly faced when she experienced two minor strokes two days apart. Despite being in the middle of three speaking gigs across the country and running a $1.5 million company, life literally stopped on a dime for her.

Sitting in the hospital and learning that she had a 60 percent chance of having a full stroke within a year, Nichole took stock of her life. Life wasn't easy for Nichole while growing up. Her father had committed suicide when she was nine and she was molested and raped as a teen. There was no financial security in her family, and Nichole constantly felt as if she weren't good enough in many areas of her life. Once she left home, however, she was driven to succeed. She started a social media company that became wildly successful, but it wasn't enough.

Lying in the hospital bed, Nichole admitted defeat. She had been on an uphill grind for so long that the stress was monumental. She was always striving for more. Something was always missing from her life— she wanted a better body, a bigger company, more money, financial freedom—the list went on. The message she had been giving herself was that she was never good enough. She describes her existence as:

> I was chasing financial freedom and security, but I couldn't appreciate other things. I created all this success, but it wasn't relaxing. I focused on goals, and all my goals were related to security and freedom, but it was never enough; I always wanted more. I realized that if I died tomorrow, money isn't important. I didn't want to spend my last day on earth earning money—I wanted to collect experiences—not only experiences, but also being fully involved with the experiences.

Nichole looked for answers by seeking out people who were happy. She turned to a business coach she had hired when she started her company. He was the happiest person she knew, but ironically, he didn't have a house, a job, or financial security; yet money always appeared for him and he traveled the world. "I want what you have—that happiness," she told him.

The first thing he had Nichole do was to face all the bad experiences of her past and to let go of all the negative experiences in her life. Her constant thoughts of not being good enough—those were negative. She had to let go of them and learn to see herself, and life, in a whole new way.

"He taught me how to clear all the triggers," Nichole explained. "I went through a five-month process of facing every trigger and all the negative experiences in my life. I faced it all until there was nothing left. That was the first time I felt truly free."

Nichole shared with me how her transformation occurred:

I learned to look in the mirror and say, "I love myself. I don't want to change anything."

We are constantly comparing ourselves to others and we try to fit into other people's standards. I came to realize those standards are other people's issues, their things they need to handle, and they're not related to me or how I feel. I gave up trying to fit in. I felt so free. Now I do whatever I want.

Loving yourself is a wonderful gift. Many of us feel scared to love ourselves. We have a fear we aren't good enough. It's really wonderful when you get into a place where you feel content. I don't need other people or other things; I'm perfect just the way I am. I don't need to change myself; I'm perfect already.

I'm working on a new module, "The Game We Play in Business." We hide our trauma. When you know the games, then you actually see all around you that every person you meet is playing this game. They don't even know they're playing it. It's coming from a space of doing the right thing to do. I've identified sixteen games, and I teach others how to end the games.

One of the things important to finding your passion is recognizing the games you play. Every game is played by either heroes, villains, or victims. The secret to happiness is to get rid of the games you're playing, creating a passionate, "Hell, yes" life, and being fully present in today.

Passion truly lights you up inside. You can feel it inside your body—it's energy that's like nothing else.

Today, Nichole feels fortunate that she's been given a chance to live her life in a very different way. She makes decisions with an entirely new set of criteria. If a decision isn't a passionate "Hell, yes!" then Nichole lets it go.

"When you live your life in a place of fear energy," she concludes, "you will create things from fear, but when you live from faith energy, you realize life is a fairy tale and you are the designer of that fairy tale."

The Five-Year Test

The Five-Year Test is nothing new. Companies have been using it as a standard interview question to determine how passionate and goal-oriented a new hire might be.

The activity is a simple one:

Fast forward five years from now. What do you want to be doing? What kind of life do you envision yourself having five years from now?

Take a moment to write out your vision for the future:

Now let's take a look at the path you're on today. Let's pause for a minute and imagine that five years from now, you're having the exact same life that you have today.

Would that be okay?

No?

Why not?

Are you at the same job? Are you hanging out with the same people? Are you having the same experiences? The same vacations? Or lack of?

If you're recoiling in horror at the idea of being stuck in the same old place five years later, then let me say this:

If you do not make conscious changes today, you will continue down the same path that you're on right now.

Five years will go by and you'll be that person at the party who has the same song, different year.

Changes do not have to be big to have an impact. Small changes and little tweaks can add up. Let's take television for example. Watching TV tends to be a *huge* time suck for many people. You can tweak your time during each day and shift your focus in the joyful direction you truly want to go in. Figure out what your time-suckers are, knock them out of your life, and replace them with something you're passionate about. I promise you'll thank me, five years later.

Bestselling author Jerry B. Jenkins wrote 187 books. Read that again. One Hundred and Eighty-Seven books. In the beginning of his writing career, he worked a full-time job, came home, spent quality time with his three boys and his wife, and finally, sat down to write from 9 p.m. until midnight.

Every night.

Jerry gave up TV and chose to work on something he was passionate about. I'm pretty sure he's not sad about missing the re-runs of *That '70s Show*.

Amy Guth: Multiple Passions Equal a Passionate Life

When people come up to Amy Guth and ask, "What do you do?" there's no easy answer at first. Amy wears many hats and has a list that reads a mile long. She's an author, journalist, TV host, radio host—and usually has several projects going at once.

"I think many people have the mis-perception that I'm not clear," Amy said. "I'm really clear about why I'm doing what I do and what it is that I want to accomplish. When I go into a new thing, I know what success looks like and I know what I want to accomplish. I let the 'how' surprise me. When I get to the goal, then new opportunities keep opening up."

Amy had a crystal clear vision of her life since she was a young girl. When she was seven, her parents gave her a pretty, blue typewriter, so Amy immediately started printing her own news. She spent her time playing in front of cameras with a microphone in hand. Amy didn't make a grand decision to go down the journalism route—it was simply something she always wanted to do.

"For me, life is a brick wall—many different bricks make up the wall of my life," Amy explained. "All of these bricks are what I love to do—writing my first book, working for the *Chicago Tribune*, founding a Literary Festival—it's a wonderful blank canvas. When I've had a vision for a bigger cause or the freedom to build my own road—that's when I thrive the most."

Of all the people I talked to for this book, I believe Amy has the most interesting view of passion. To Amy, passion is honesty. "I believe passion is related to authenticity," she said. "We all have things that move us, that are dear to our heart, to act on that—it's your truth, your gift to the world."

Sadly, Amy told me, fear is the enemy of passion. Fear will block passion. If you don't pursue something that impacts your heart, if you don't go for something you're passionate about, there's always regret.

Amy learned the lesson of urgency in life at a very young age. When she was five, a close family member died in a car accident. "She was young, creative, and very spirited," Amy said. "And she was gone in an instant. We think it will never happen to us—that's why there's nothing to be gained by putting things off."

Of course, it's difficult as heck even to think that you could face the end of your life in an instant or much sooner than you'd like, but the realization that you're living on borrowed time could be the catalyst you need to let go of the stuff that isn't serving you anymore and to focus on creating a life that does.

When it comes to passion, Amy has more to say:

When passion is right, it feels good. It's important to be honest with yourself—if it doesn't feel good, stop. Move on. Passion is about being authentic and real.

We don't have to have everything figured out to passionately pursue what we love to do. Our lives are a blank canvas. If it's not what you want, have the courage to change it no matter how hard it is.

I think the reason people accept mediocrity is because of fear. Every experience shapes who we are. Our reactions shape us. Sometimes, fearful reactions stop us.

Many people are afraid—they feel they don't have the answers. The fear of being wrong, that's what holds people back. People want to wait until they can do it perfectly—that's the enemy, being perfect. People say, "I wish...I wish...but now I'm old." There are terrible stories of people who put off their passions—they don't grab that chance. That's why the word, "NOW" is powerful—passion is urgency.

A Few Things You Won't Say at the End of Your Life:

- I'm really glad I spent all that time worrying about the things that never happened.
- I'm so happy I remodeled the downstairs bathroom four times.
- All those arguments I won against my spouse were really worth it.
- I'm glad I kept the entire china set so sparkling new by never using it.
- It's a good thing I ran all those errands every day.

- I really wish I spent more time in the malls shopping for stuff I don't need.

What are some things you're focusing on now that won't really matter in the long run...or at the end of your life journey? (Come on; let's be brutally honest here. Write 'em down.)

_____

_____

_____

_____

_____

_____

_____

CHAPTER 11

Discovering Passion Through Meditation

"You should sit in meditation for twenty minutes every day—unless you're too busy. Then you should sit for an hour."
~ **Zen proverb**

Whenever I'm running on spin cycle and life becomes a muddled mess, the greatest antidote is...quiet time.

I'm the first to admit that this is where being deaf becomes an advantage. Whenever I seek out quiet time, I shut off my hearing aids and presto: silence.

In this busy world, sometimes it feels counterproductive to stop everything and meditate, but that quiet time is the catalyst for your passions and for forward movement in your life. In fact, it is that very busyness that blocks out the intuitive guidance within you. By deliberately carving out time to sit in meditative silence, you'll find a wealth of information and answers instead. My daughter and I recently experienced a ninety-minute silent meditation with a group of women. There's something powerful about being in a room meditating with others. (For one thing, you can't leave!) I brought along a notebook, and to my surprise, I ended up jotting down answers to questions that had been lingering in my mind for a while.

For me, nature restores my soul. I love to meditate when I'm surrounded by beautiful landscapes. If I'm unable to have quiet time in a beautiful place, I use images on my phone or computer to put myself in a wonderful state of mind before I become still.

Worry: The Passion Sapper

When you spend time deep in worry, you trade your today for an unpromised tomorrow. Worry robs you of enjoying the very moment you have now. Worry is wasted energy. Worrying about tomorrow or reflecting obsessively about the past robs you of living today to the fullest.

Your attitude and your energy are like a magnet. What you put out is what comes drawn back to you. While an occasional "woe is me" moment can draw support, a continuous feed of pity can scatter people away.

My mother is the biggest worrier I know, yet ironically, she and my father taught me one of the best lessons about worry.

I purchased a Jet Ski one summer. Then one fall weekend, I planned to winterize the watercraft.

The problem was, I had no clue what to do. When I read the instruction manual, it might as well have been written in Greek. As the weekend wore on, the stress was beginning to affect me physically. My neck was aching and my jaw was tense. I decided to drive to the local marine shop and get some advice. My mom came along for the ride.

We talked about a bunch of things, and ironically, the topic of stress came up.

"Remember that piece of advice you gave me a long time ago? You told me that you used to worry and be stressed out, and then you realized you were wasting a lot of time worrying."

My mom nodded. "Yes, everything always has a way of working out; it just always does, so why get all worked up about it?" she said. "I look back at all the years that I was stressed out about something or other—I didn't have to worry so much."

So throughout the years, I've tried to remember Mom's words when I find myself deep in worry. I have to ask myself these questions:

- What is the solution?
- What is the worst possible thing that could happen?
- What can I change right now to ease the way I feel?

When I arrived back home, my dad helped me winterize the Jet Ski using the instructions I had received from the marine mechanic.

"I just hope I did this right," I told my dad as we wheeled it into the storage shed.

"Well, no use worrying about it," he said. "We'll find out in the spring."

(The Jet Ski started up perfectly every year!)

So, what's the antidote to worry?

Meditation.

Now, before you roll your eyes at this practice, hear me out.

In our go-go-go culture, the practice of being quiet and still often seems out of place. Yet, in the quiet stillness, that's where you find answers to your most pressing life questions. Meditation isn't about eliminating your thoughts; in fact, you may find yourself having so many creative thoughts that it's difficult to put them out of your mind. The more you practice meditation, the more you "lean in" to your thoughts, your feelings, your awareness, your breath, and your presence.

Every now and then, I kick off my shoes and walk barefoot on a path or through the grass. I also take the time out to watch the sunset. Even though I live in a suburb of Chicago, I always manage to find places where I can restore my energy through nature. Outside, in the fresh air, you'll find negative ions (which are a positive thing!), especially around moving water or in the mountains. In fact, Howard Partridge credits the beach for being the best place for discovering new, passionate ideas.

Be Present, Now

Stop reading this book for a moment. Just be. As I write these words, I've paused to look around me. I'm on an airplane, staring at the seat in front of me. I look out the window, thankful that I can see the fluffy, white clouds that look like frosting on a cake. I can feel the warmth of the sun streaming through the glass in sharp contrast to the cold that is swirling around me. I'm filled with gratitude. I'm alive. I'm breathing. I'm about to embark on another adventure.

Five years ago, I didn't practice awareness on this level. I was rushing through life meeting sales numbers and juggling too many tasks at once. I actually probably have even more on my plate today, but because

I take the time to reflect, ponder, and meditate, I am so much more appreciative instead.

"When you're deep in your passion, you're fully present in that moment," Debbie Leoni told me. Debbie is the owner of Fearless Living, and she hosts retreats to challenge people to face the very things that are holding them back in fear.

"As children," Debbie explains, "we already know how to experience passion, happiness, and joy. We've been conditioned as adults to forget that—we don't give ourselves permission to feel. Passion doesn't arrive at the door for us—we have to reveal the passion that's already within us."

Fear is a big factor that robs us from being fully in the present. We have to determine what fear is costing us—what is the price we are paying to remain wrapped in fear instead of moving forward?

Action is the answer, Debbie told me. "Moving away from fear requires taking action in place of fear—and being willing to take a risk."

Restore and Recharge

It's essential to allow for quiet time during your day to restore and recharge. Meditation brings ideas and answers to any questions you may have. Bring a spiral notebook or blank journal with you to jot down ideas, thoughts, or revelations that occur during your meditative practice. It is the silence between notes that make music, and it is the silence between thoughts that brings about the most tranquil, meditative state.

CHAPTER 12

Mastering Your Passion

"If you want to be happy, set a goal that commands your thoughts, liberates your energy, and inspires your hope."
~ **Andrew Carnegie**

Y ou've probably heard this before: It takes 10,000 hours to master something.

This is not true for everything. You can experience mastery in a shorter amount of time when you are lined up with your purpose, and you can shorten your learning time even more with teachers, coaches, and mentors leading the way.

There are days when the 10,000-hour mastery process is both a good and bad thing:

- "Oh, I haven't put in the 10,000 hours to master what I want to do." (I'll keep trying.)
- "Oh gosh, I have 9,364 more hours before I can master this...." (I want to give up.)

Ten thousand hours translates to ten years.

Ten. Years.

But think of it this way: The 10,000 hours of mastery is a journey. If you're going to put in 10,000 hours to master something, how much more fulfilling and joyful will it be if it's...

- Something you're passionate about.
- Something that is lined up with your gifts and skills.
- Something you were born to do.

That's why passion matters. It's the fuel that carries you through the hours and hours of mastery. How much more enjoyable and fun something becomes when you are passionately, madly in love with what you want to do.

My work frequently takes me to new places and I'm always sharing those photos on social media. Sometimes people are confused. "It seems like you're always on vacation," one person remarked. When work and play are blended and you enjoy what you do, then every day becomes a vacation. That's what Seth Godin is referring to when he says, "Instead of wondering when your next vacation is, maybe you should set up a life you don't need to escape from."

The Messy Middle

There's a learning curve when you are doing something that's totally new to you. Every expert on earth has started out as a beginner. I often tell people, "Don't compare your beginning to someone else's ten-year process."

In the six years of exploring the topic of passion, I've come across many stories of people who bailed out—in the middle. The work became too hard. The cost seemed too great. The fear overtook them.

There's a price that comes with leaving a passionate path too soon: regret. This is why clarity is important—when you are clear about your passion and purpose, you will keep that front and center, even when the journey gets rough in the middle of it all.

Brené Brown calls this process "Day Two," something she learned through hosting three-day workshops. The first day, everyone is excited and running on high energy. By Day Two, everything slips. The work is deep, the energy is lower, and suddenly, not everything is fun anymore.

In her book, *Rising Strong*, Brené believes that the messy middle is necessary—it's the place where the magic begins. "Day Two, or whatever that middle space is for your own process, is when you're 'in the dark'— the door has closed behind you. You're too far in to turn around and not close enough to the end to see the light."

The messy middle is where many people give up, but for those who stay the course, the middle brings you to the triumphant place in your journey where you see all the pieces fitting together.

Mike McAleese, a Hall of Fame Massage Therapist, faced the messy middle with his quest to complete an Ironman Triathlon. Mike told me his story while taping up a couple of muscles that I strained while barefoot water skiing. His passion is triathlons and he wanted to conquer the ultimate one: an Ironman.

Mike invested in good equipment and trained for a year. On the morning of the Ironman Wisconsin, his confidence fell. The temperature was in the low 50s and large swells covered the lake.

Mike recalled his wife and trainer's advice to practice swimming in rough water—advice he largely ignored. During the first mile, fifty-two-year old Mike began to doubt his ability to finish. He was swallowing water and throwing up. Halfway through the grueling swim, Mike gave up. He hung on to the rescue kayak, gasping for breath. When he arrived on the shore, he could see disappointment etched on the faces of his wife and training coach. Mike was filled with regret, but he vowed to finish the next Ironman he entered.

"I needed to do it. I just had to finish an Ironman," Mike said. "So I trained harder. I swam in the rough waters of Lake Michigan."

There was a big smile on Mike's face when he saw the flat lake water at his second Ironman. His wife, Star, and his best friend Tom were cheering him along when he emerged from the water.

Fifty miles into the bike race, a severe migraine slowed him down. Mike was battling the doubt demons inside.

"Mike, I love you, but don't you dare give up," Tom told him. "If you give up, I'm going to beat the crap out of you!"

Mike's wife gave him chocolate and some Tylenol. Thirteen miles into running the last leg of the race, blisters began popping up. Mike switched to walking. "I was okay with Plan B," he said. "When Plan A doesn't work out, there's always twenty-five other letters in the alphabet."

With his wife by his side, Mike hobbled through the last few miles and then crossed the finish line in triumph.

In a sad turn of events, his best friend Tom was killed in an accident. Mike carried Tom with him for his third Ironman, stopping to spread his ashes during the bike race. Halfway through the running, Mike's leg began to cramp up. Once again, doubt crept in. "You have to believe in yourself," his wife urged him. The next thing he knew, his phone began to ring with texts from friends urging him to keep going. Mike finished the Ironman with just five minutes to spare.

To get through the messy middle, Mike believes you have to have passion, faith, and a vision to guide you. Support from others is important, for everyone needs encouragement to get through the messy, tough parts.

Filling the Gap

So how can you fill the gap between where you are now and where you passionately want to be?

The shortcut is to learn and surround yourself with people who are living the passion you're seeking. So ask yourself this:

- Who is living the life you want? Who is doing the things you want to do? Who has achieved what you're seeking?
- What can you do or experience that will bring you closer to your passions?
- Who can you add to your team—who are the people who will push you, mentor you, and teach you?
- Who can you ask for help, for assistance, for guidance, and for wisdom?

How Personality Plays a Part

In the process of writing this book, I put out a request on the HARO (Help a Reporter Out) website asking to interview people on the topic of passion.

Marie O'Riordan and Naoise O'Reilly from Ireland responded to me. The two of them specialize in understanding the psychology behind success in business and in life, using a process called Purple Psychology. Their message is simple: Everyone can be successful if they understand and work with their natural abilities.

"Everyone has a dream. We take people through a process and pull it out of them—and show them what they can become," Marie said. "Sometimes there is a lot of pressure to follow a path in life that physically and mentally is not what they want—we help guide them to what they were born to be. Traditional psychologists are obsessed with what makes a person tick; we are obsessed with the factors that create a person's personality or how to be *you*."

Marie and Naoise are no strangers to passion—they each set out to create joyful lives from a very young age, despite personal challenges. Marie struggled in school with an auditory processing disorder, but when she was a teenager, she began working at a radio station and then moved on to TV. She studied journalism in college and worked in media. Naoise had dyslexia, which the school psychologists didn't diagnose until years later. She tape-recorded her lessons and didn't read her first book until she was thirteen.

Naoise wanted to become a doctor but settled for becoming a marine scientist instead. While she was in college, she set up services to help deaf and disabled students, and in the process, she discovered different ways to assist students with learning. Despite her own continual challenges with dyslexia, Naoise achieved her Ph.D., something many of her teachers couldn't fathom while she struggled in school.

Marie and Naoise crossed paths in 2012 and formed a business helping others of all ages achieve their very best through their own unique learning system. "We wanted to spread the message that all people can be successful," Naoise said.

Between the two of them, they've racked up many awards for their work, but that's not what drives them. They love everything they do and life itself is a passion. They are firm believers in living with intent. When she was four years old, Marie created a bucket list with over 200 items on it—including meeting Paul Newman and Mother Teresa. In fact, at age twenty-two, Marie produced a documentary on Mother Teresa and conducted the last interview that Mother Teresa ever gave before her death. By the time Marie turned thirty-three, she had completed all the items on her list.

Naoise and Marie often work with Olympic athletes, and they can quickly see results with their approach. The factor that motivates people is often related to an emptiness they're trying to fill. No two people are the same, and personality plays a role in unlocking success. "Ninety-nine percent of winning in sports is related to psychology," Marie explained. "If you're successful in your brain, you will be successful in the body."

"It's great to have a passion—and for someone to successfully do something, their personality plays a role," Naoise said. "People are two sides of a coin—heads is all the good stuff, when they're happy in their best situation. The other side is negative, how they behave when things are not going well, or not working the best way, or the environment doesn't suit them. It's not just about what you want to do or your passion, it's also about how you do it to become successful at it."

During the interview and afterwards, Naoise and Marie mentioned they felt I had a rare personality type. Curious, I decided to take a personality test. Sure enough, the results pointed toward INFJ (introverted, intuitive, feeling, judging)—a personality type that is shared by just 1 percent of the population.

Suddenly, many things clicked into place. All the years I spent struggling to "fit in," of feeling like a square peg in a round hole, suddenly all of that made sense. In the last several years, I've learned to do the opposite—to lean in to who I am and to line myself up with my strengths.

Personality tests are often used by corporations to put people in a nice, neat little box and predict outcomes based on personality profiles. Ironically, the original personality tests were designed with the intention of bringing out individuality, not mass results.

Bill Schultz: An Ultra-Passion for Running

"Pick a goal, then do the work."

That's the life strategy that sixty-four-year-old Bill Schultz lives by. Bill loves to run. He started running in 1978 and hasn't stopped since. To say he's passionate is putting it mildly. Some might call him obsessed.

Bill's passion for ultra-distance running began innocently enough in 1981 when achieving the feeling of success that comes from longer and further distances became a personal accomplishment for him. Soon, he was setting records in long distance races. In 1990, Bill took a leave of absence from his job as a fifth-grade teacher to run across the United States. He didn't have sponsors. He didn't have a lofty cause to stand behind. Bill ran not only as a test for himself, but also for his students. One of Bill's lessons to his students is: If you do the homework and prepare well, the test is easy.

"Many adults tell kids, 'Try to do your best; you can do it,' but kids don't always see others doing that or their parents doing that," Bill said. "I didn't just want to say those words to my students—I wanted to show that I could do it."

Bill's journey began in California by dipping a toe in the Pacific Ocean to touch off his personal race. He estimated it would take him 100 days to reach the East Coast. He had no doubt in his mind he would succeed. He was logging over 4,000 miles a year and had previously set an American record at a six-day race. "I was prepared physically, mentally, and emotionally," Bill said. "I interviewed people, looked at charts, and did a lot of work to prepare. Once I left the West Coast, I put my right foot forward, then my left, and repeated it."

"Being passionate about something means you're willing to be vested in it through all the ups and downs."
~ Bill Schultz

Ninety-five days later, Bill put his foot in the Atlantic Ocean and triumphantly celebrated the completion of his cross-country dream.

And Bill continued to run.

Seven years ago, Bill (a vegetarian for thirty years) was sidelined by double bypass surgery. Running was the last thing on his mind while being wheeled into surgery. "I was thinking about living," Bill said. "If I could run again, that was a bonus."

Once Bill recovered, he was hitting the pavement again, one foot after another. At the age of sixty-two, the seasoned competitor set a record at the Six Day race in his age division.

During a recent, routine checkup, Bill learned that his blood test showed a compromised immune system. Despite this new health challenge, Bill continues to run.

"To achieve success," Bill told me, "you have to pick an attainable goal and get it—that's different than a dream—a dream is something you *wish* you could do. With a goal, you can write down how to achieve it—step one, two, three, and four. If something comes up, you have to back up and do 3a or 3b again or go around to achieve it. Keep the carrot in front of the donkey. There's nothing like success, even small successes. If someone is trying to lose weight and he loses one pound, that's success."

Bill is aiming for his 1,000-mile recognition at the next Six Day race. As long as he can, he intends to enjoy his passion to run. What fuels him in every aspect of his life is a five-line piece of inspiration he coined:

May the sun forever shine upon your face.

May the wind forever blow upon your back.

May your goals forever be in sight.

May your beliefs forever give you strength.

May your spirit forever run free.

CHAPTER 13

Living Someone Else's Life

"Your vision will become clear only when you look into your heart. Who looks outside, dreams. Who looks inside, awakens."
~ Carl Jung

D
o you feel like you're living someone else's life, a life designed by other people?

Jack Canfield, co-author of the Chicken Soup for the Soul series, believes you are born with a purpose, so it's your obligation to discover your gifts and give them to the world.

In his book, *The Success Principles*, Jack shares: "A life of purpose is not only a true expression of who you really are—it is your gift to the world—and the world needs what you have to offer. When you are living your life 'on purpose,' you will find greater fulfillment and joy in all that you do."

Stop living someone else's life or dreams for you. Passion is highly personal. Only *you* know your own thoughts, feelings, emotions, reactions, and outcomes when it comes to passion.

From the time you were very young, you were inundated with rules. You were taught to do this, not that.

I never thought twice about taking my kids out of school for an adventure or a vacation. To me, those times were more precious than anything they would have learned in school. One year when the kids missed quite a bit of school, I received a letter from the state warning of impending truancy if the kids missed any more days of instruction. I just had to laugh. My kids learned far more from their experiences and our time together as a family. The oldest kid graduated from college with an economics degree, the middle kid performed on Broadway, and the youngest is in college. The missed days of school were worth it—because to this day, they remember the life lessons from the guy they met flying a kite on the beach, the bike ride we took on Hilton Head island with the alligators on the road, and the trips we shared with other families.

> *"Passion is born when you begin to get a glimpse of your possibilities."*
> ~ Zig Ziglar

Pete Gluszek: A Passion for Fishing

Remember the guy I introduced at the beginning of this book—the one who was reading a book next to me on the plane about how to turn your passion into profit?

Meet Pete Gluszek.

Pete's passion for fishing goes all the way back to when he was a toddler. His father used to take him fishing on a small pond in Oxhill, Maryland. At age four, Pete discovered a love for the outdoors on Broad Creek, one of the Potomac River's tributaries.

"I don't know what it was about fishing, but I loved it," Pete recalled. "I wanted to do it more than anything. It was exciting to me—the thrill of the catch. I wanted to go fishing; that's what I remember. I wanted to fish the rest of my life."

Pete fished every chance he could get. The first time he went fishing in a boat, he caught a large-mouthed bass. Right then and there, he knew that was the fish he wanted to catch each time.

"As soon as we had a break from school, I would go fishing alone or with my friends. I find the same enjoyment alone or with people—something about the outdoors is so peaceful—both the quiet and the excitement. If I can share it, great. If I'm alone, it is also good. The passion is definitely there."

During Pete's senior year in high school, one of his friends came over with a fully-loaded tackle box. It was the first time Pete had ever seen such an assortment of lures, hooks, bobbers, and more. They studied the habits and patterns of large-mouth bass and became self-taught experts.

Pete went off to college to study environmental engineering, but his heart was still centered firmly on fishing. He turned down parties so he could get up early the next morning to head out to a local lake.

While at a graduation party, Pete discovered there was a Bass Club, and several members were talking about an upcoming fishing tournament the following weekend. Pete was floored. He had no idea this kind of utopia existed. (This was long before the Internet, young readers!)

"I didn't know any of the fishing terms they used, but I asked questions and learned the basics," Pete recalled. "I was so excited—this was on a lake that I fished on all the time."

Some of the best fishermen in the state were registered for the tournament. Pete showed up with basic equipment and a heavy dose of naiveté—he didn't know the rules nor the formats for measuring fish.

But he had two things to his advantage: an intense passion for catching bass and knowledge about how to catch them in that lake.

"We destroyed everyone; second place was not even in the ball park," Pete said. "We won $600—that felt like a million dollars. It was an awesome experience."

Pete was hooked. (Oh, yes, pun intended.) He took a job as an environmental engineer and continued to enter every tournament he could. He read every fishing magazine he could find. He wasn't interested in TV; he was consumed by his passion for bass and wanted to learn everything he could about the sport. He used his two weeks of vacation one year to enter one of the top tournaments, the Bass Invitational. He came in 156th place out of 300 anglers.

"I made a lot of mistakes, but it was eye-opening," Pete said. "You have no appreciation for winning if you don't lose—you drive yourself to the next level when you lose."

At the next tournament, Pete came in second. That wasn't too shabby, considering the prize was $5,000 and a fully-rigged bass boat!

Pete went on to beat some seasoned fishermen in tournament after tournament. Then one day, he started playing with the idea of turning fishing into a career. He was ranked among the top 100 anglers in the country. Despite a well-paying job, Pete knew his destiny was not engineering. Sitting at a desk all day was not the way he wanted to spend his life; he was living each day for the moment he could get outside and fish.

Pete was at a crossroads. He was about to take his professional engineering exam. He felt it was impossible to work as an engineer and compete full-time with the best anglers. He was searching for an opportunity to leave his job and dive into the sport completely—doing the work he truly loved. It was a 180-degree change to chase something that no one thought was possible.

"The doubts were there, I had to learn how to break through—there are no shortcuts; it's about effort, intensity, and focus," Pete said. "People think you have to have talent, but it's about your work ethic and your drive."

Leaving a secure job and steady paycheck was scary—Pete's emotions were all over the place. Pete maxed out his credit cards that first year, but the sense of freedom and excitement were worth it, as he explains:

> After all those years in school and at work, all of a sudden I could commit 110 percent to my passion at the highest level. It was daunting and very difficult with no sponsors, no financial security, but the passion was something you can't even imagine.
>
> Every Monday morning, I would wake up early just like when I was in engineering, but my desk was a bass boat. I would pass all the cars going to work the daily grind that I had just escaped. My new life was on the lake, watching the sun come up every day. That is a pleasure, an enjoyment that is indescribable, something that I have never taken for granted for the last fifteen years. Every Monday morning, when I go to my office, I get a sense of excitement that is like no other.

Today, you can find Pete on TV and in magazines, sharing his passion with others. He also runs Bass University, teaching others how to snag the big catches.

"People always look at dreams and say, 'It's not for me; it's for someone else,'" Peter says. "But when you follow your passion you will be better at that than anyone else. You work long hours, but it's not work, you would do it anyway. It's a fantastic feeling!"

CHAPTER 14

Stumbling Along the Journey

"There are no mistakes, no coincidences. All events are blessings given to us to learn from."
~ **Elizabeth Kubler-Ross**

Sometimes, to get to the right decision, you have to make the wrong one. I learned this lesson through my work with Hands & Voices, a parent-driven organization that provides support for families with deaf and hard of hearing children. All three of my kids are deaf/hard of hearing. In the beginning stages of parenthood, I stumbled with many choices, paths, and experiences until I got into a place where things began to feel and be right. There were times when the choices were clearly not working, leading me to explore a different path and a different choice.

Many people go through life thinking of 1,000 reasons why something won't work out instead of seeing the incredible rewards if it does work out. So they never try. They never take the leap. They never know the ecstatic feeling that comes from going through the trials into tribulations.

I met Candace Bui-Walston at a women's networking event. At first, we had some difficulty communicating because I had trouble lip-reading through her Chinese accent, but I saw passion in her eyes.

"Let's talk," I said.

So Candace shared her story. Her family had moved from China when Candace was in high school. Life was not going well in China— Candace was struggling in school and failing many of her classes. The move would be a clean slate—a chance to start over again. Yet Candace faced a big challenge: She knew very little English.

"My older sister and I went to explore the neighborhood and we became lost," Candace said. "We walked into a McDonald's to get drinks, and we didn't know what 'small, medium, or large' meant. We decided we had to learn English to survive, so we focused on learning fast."

Candace was so successful in picking up the language that she obtained her Bachelor's and Master's degrees. She worked as a teacher and then became an assistant principal. As time went on, Candace began to struggle with the educational system's politics and she started dreading her work week.

During one teacher evaluation, Candace's supervisor instructed her to turn in a positive review. Based on her professional observation as the assistant principal, she felt the teacher's performance was poor and the outcome was reflected in the students' lack of progress. Candace knew she could not create an evaluation that went against her own values.

"At that point, I couldn't do it anymore," Candace said. "I decided to leave. I was juggling too much, and I wasn't happy. I felt if I couldn't give 100 percent, I shouldn't be there."

The decision was easy, but walking away from a six-figure income was a challenge. At first, Candace panicked, but she had a small tutoring business on the side that brought in some income.

As she scouted around for jobs, Candace started noticing that she was enjoying the tutoring process more and more. Every time a student left happy, the feeling filled a place in her heart. She decided to stop looking for jobs and expand her business instead.

"Until the past year, I never knew what passion meant to me," Candace said. "To me, it means I love what I'm doing. I'm able to use my knowledge to do what I love and also benefit other people. I'm not making a six-figure income today, but I love what I'm doing and I'm happy. I'm able to do what I want to do and teach what I want to teach. I'm home with my children. If you follow your passion, the money will come. I'm now seeing many students, and I was offered a teaching position at a university. I feel that following my passion led me to a better place."

A friend once told me, "There are no failures, only lessons." What a beautiful way to look at life. Our stumbles and struggles are lessons on our journey.

CHAPTER 15

Waiting for Permission

*"Don't wait for the next thing—
make the next thing happen!"*
~ **Banana George,** *World's Oldest
Barefoot Water Skier*

W hen my daughter called me to tell me she was dropping out of
college in her freshman year, my heart sank. She was walking away
from a film scholarship at a college that I thought was perfect for
her.

I was wrong.

She was completely miserable going to classes. She had struggled
with school beginning in fourth grade—and the thought of sitting in

classes for another three years gave her a trapped feeling. She wanted to become an actor in front of the camera, not behind it.

Yet the parent in me wanted to see her get a degree. "Just stay, have fun for the next three years, grab the degree, and then you can go out and do whatever you want," I said.

"How can you tell others to follow their passions when you can't even let your own daughter do that?" she replied.

She was right.

I called her back the next day (she tells me it was actually a few days later) and gave her my support. After the semester ended, she moved back home to figure out her next steps. Halfway through the summer, she expressed some frustration at not knowing what would be next.

And silly me, I said, "Well, you can always go back to college...."

I was scared for her. The parent in me was having a big internal argument with the Passion Mentor in me.

Then an audition popped up for a Broadway play—the same play my husband and I had prevented her from trying out for the year before so she could go to college instead. She booked a flight to New York City to try out for a swing role in the play. When she FaceTimed me to tell me she got the part, the happiness on her face was priceless. She's now living the Broadway life in New York. The greatest moment came when she stepped on stage and passionately performed in front of a sold-out audience.

And Mom?

She learned a lesson.

"There's two reasons why people don't do things. One is they tell themselves they can't do them, or people around them tell them they can't do them. Either way, we start to believe it. Either we give up, or we never start in the first place."
~ **Scott Dinsmore**, *Live Your Legend*

Other People's Influence

In his book, *How Did I Get Here?: The Ascent of an Unlikely CEO*, pro skateboarder Tony Hawk gave this advice: "Once you find your passion, run with it. Ignore what peers or career counselors say." He goes on to share this: "If your passion is dismissed as mainstream and dorky, that makes your insurgency all the braver. Do it because you love it, not because you're worried about what others—teachers, friends, that hot emo chick who sits alone by the bike rack at lunch—will think."

Shortly after I became deaf, I was sitting with a career counselor at college and going over my options. As a sophomore, it was time for me to figure out the direction of my life and decide on a major.

"I'm thinking of nursing," I said. I loved babies. I imagined myself working in the labor and delivery unit, handing newborn babies over to the parents.

The concerned look on the counselor's face threw me off.

"What if you misunderstand a doctor or patient? How will you use the phone? Communication will be a challenge."

So I thought about taking up computer programming or accounting—the two things my mom suggested, which were guaranteed to bring me a steady job with good pay. But my heart sank at the idea of doing either of those things.

I picked counseling. It was the one thing that matched up to my skills. I really didn't know what I was getting into, nor did I realize that I would need to get a Master's degree to go into Rehabilitation Counseling. I just kind of fell into it.

By the beginning of graduate school, I felt like I was making a mistake. I wanted to quit, but I rationalized I was too far into the program to walk away. Every time I expressed my desire to quit to a friend, she poured on the encouragement and pulled me along. I decided I would just grit through it and get the degree.

If you're externally-driven, it's all too easy to fall prey to other people's influences on your life choices. You'll sway like a loose sail in the wind, turning every which way, but not following a path that's true for you.

> *"Let the beauty of what you love be what you do."*
> ~ Rumi

You Don't Need Permission

By the time I graduated from college, I knew I didn't want a job in Rehabilitation Counseling, the very major I had studied for. I took a different job, instead. Four years into the job, I decided to explore some options in the medical field. The lure of working with babies in labor and delivery was still there, but being deaf, the communication struggle was still very real. There was no way for me to use the telephone except through a cumbersome relay system that was extremely slow.

I started exploring the idea of becoming an Ultrasound Tech. I figured it was the perfect path for me—allowing me to work with babies in an environment where I could handle the communication aspects.

Then I hit upon an idea: I called the local hospital and arranged to job shadow an Ultrasound Tech to see the action firsthand.

It was the best three hours of my life.

Because, you see, at the end of the third hour, I knew the medical field was not the path for me. I sat through several ultrasounds and talked with the director of Nuclear Medicine. Three hours saved me from going down yet another path that wasn't right for me, a path that didn't include my heart.

I still wanted to work with babies, so I ended up volunteering at the hospital and taking care of boarder babies.

Years later, I became a doula and had the honor of attending several hospital and home births. I loved every birth! While I was going down that path, I met deaf and hard of hearing doctors and, yes, nurses.

Yet, in hindsight, I'm thankful I didn't go down the nursing path. To this day, I can't stand needles or handling body fluids!

"You have to take risks. We will only understand the miracle of life fully when we allow the unexpected to happen."
~ Paulo Coelho

I see a lot of people waiting to begin doing what they really want to do. They wish. They plan. They consult. They prepare.

But they never begin.

In some cases, they're waiting for permission. For someone to push them. For someone to guide them. Or for someone to say, "Go. Do this."

You do not need permission to live a passionate life.

CHAPTER 16

Changing Course

> *"If one dream should fall and break
> into a thousand pieces, never be
> afraid to pick up one of those pieces
> and begin again."*
> ~ Flavia Weedn

This is where I want to move."

I stared at my mom in disbelief. We were on our way down to Florida and had stopped at an adult-living community in Nashville. The moment we walked into a model home that was for sale, everything changed on a dime. Just like that, my eighty-six-year-old mom and my sister decided to sell their house in Michigan and move to a brand new state—to a community where they knew no one.

Just like that.

On one hand, this move was a long time coming. Not long after my father passed away, my mother and sister expressed a desire to move. To where, they weren't sure. They just knew the winters at the lake were long and isolating; it was time to move on and downsize to a smaller place.

We contemplated a few different places, but nothing felt quite right. Nothing, that is, until they walked into the house in Nashville. We looked at a few other homes after that, but their hearts were set firmly and confidently on the first house. The vibe, the light, the energy—all of it tugged at their hearts.

So at eighty-six, my mom started over in a new direction. The move surprised the heck out of me, but it also taught me a valuable lesson. I've encountered so many others who have the "ageism" attitude—that they're too old to embark on anything new. I've seen this among various middle-aged friends.

"It's too late," they say. They pine away their time going in the same direction as always. What they're waiting for, I don't know, but I do know they're going to get more of the same if they stay on the same-old/same-old track.

The Power of a Pivot

In his book *The Art of Work*, Jeff Goins talks about the power of the pivot—the ability to move in a new direction from right where you are.

"Even when all other opportunities are exhausted, you can always pivot," Jeff explains. No matter the situation, people can always start right where they are in a new direction.

That's the beauty of a pivot, what seems like a starting-over point is simply a redirect, a change of course. Maybe all you need is a little tweak of direction to create the results you want. Or a complete shift of direction can be the jump-start boost you need to take off.

Not too long ago, I took up surfing for the first time. I found it exhausting, scary (I Googled the shark sightings on this beach), and exhilarating. I loved every minute of it, even when the board bounced up and hit me on the head. I managed two full rides to shore—and both times, I felt like a teenager without a care in the world.

The next day, my forty-nine-year-old body screamed in unusual places. That was perfectly okay—I figure I have quite a few years ahead of me to learn how to surf properly. Because, you see, while I was Googling the shark information, I discovered there's a whole group of older surfers out there: ninety-four-year-old John "Doc" Ball, eighty-three-year-old LeRoy "Granny" Grannis, ninety-one-year-old Woody Brown, eighty-one-year-old Rabbit Kekai...and many, many more—all out there riding the waves.

Whoa!

Didn't that just shift your whole paradigm of what it means to grow older and hang ten on your passion?

So here's what I hope you get from reading this chapter: I hope you take a good hard look at where you are today and then think about what direction you'd like to go in. Then take that step and pivot in that new direction. Learn something new. Connect with someone who can teach you what you've always wanted to learn. Go out and make a fool of yourself until you learn it.

Because you know what...? If it doesn't work out, you can simply pivot again in another direction.

> *"You have to pay attention to passion and beware of the temptation of success. It's not enough to be good at something; you must focus on what you are meant to do. And appreciate your understanding of that, over time, just might change. So be ready to make more pivots along the way."*
> ~ Jeff Goins, *The Art of Work*

You Are Not Your Past

Here's another thing that trips people up on this whole passion journey:

The past.

Major screwups, mistakes, or poor choices can feel like a noose keeping us from living the life we really want, but the reality is, we have the power to choose our thoughts and our attitude in any situation.

Ben Beeler learned this lesson the hard way. Ben and I met through a mutual business we share—SendOutCards, a greeting card and gift business.

Years ago, Ben was a drug dealer. For several years, he regularly sold cocaine and marijuana—until he was identified as a dealer and landed in a federal prison. The police had no physical evidence, nor did they catch Ben with the actual drugs; his name was simply handed over during someone else's arrest.

The minute he walked into his cell and the door closed behind him, Ben became just another uniform with a number on it. "On the second day, a fight broke out just fifteen feet from me," Ben said. "A guy was stabbed forty times from a broken pool stick, and I witnessed the whole thing. That's when reality set in—this is where I would be for the next five years of my life."

For five-and-a-half years, Ben was trapped behind bars, but he realized his mind was not. He studied law books at the prison library and used his knowledge to help other prisoners with their cases. "My conviction and arrest were based on what other people said about me," Ben explained. "They never caught me with drugs; I've never been pulled over—that was hard for me to swallow. At the time, I was operating from a very selfish mode; I didn't care about the bigger picture or seeing where I would be in ten years—all I could think about was 'How could you send me to prison based on hearsay?'"

Ben served time in four different prisons before he finally saw freedom. He was released to a halfway house while he tried to figure out what to do next and how to make a living—legally.

Who was going to hire a felon?

During his time behind bars, Ben's mom sent him positive, uplifting cards to keep his spirits up and to give him hope. When Ben was released, he joined his mom in the SendOutCards business.

Ben also turned to selling used cars and opened up his own shop. He used his card business to grow his network and referrals, until he eventually owned the number one used car business in his state.

During a SendOutCards workshop, CEO and founder Kody Bateman shared Ben's story and reminded everyone, "You can be from Yale or jail, but you are not your past."

Kody also shared a startling statistic: 87 percent of what we are exposed to every day, from the news to our experiences, is negative.

*"The stories in your mind become the
stories of your life."*
~ Kody Bateman

Ben was inspired to focus on the opposite statistic in his daily life. He created T-shirts that read: "13%." Whenever someone sees him wearing that shirt, it always sparks a conversation and leads him to even more business. It also gives him a chance to encourage others to shift their daily thoughts and actions to reflect the positive.

"Where I am today is a combination of surrounding myself with positive people and my mindset," says Ben. "One of the things I taught myself is: If I don't want to make a bad decision, if I don't put myself in a position to make a poor choice, then I couldn't make that choice."

Like Ben, you can choose to move on from your past and create a whole new future. The first step is making that conscious choice to pivot and then step forward in a new direction. Remember, once you are clear about what you want in your life and begin to take action, more and more opportunities will show up and people will step into your life.

You Don't Have to Grow Older, Just Bolder

Speaking of growing bolder, I want to introduce you to Bill Shafer and Marc Middleton. The two of them were long-time reporters for WESH station in Florida. Year after year, they dutifully read the teleprompter and delivered the news. Despite numerous awards for their work, they were growing weary of reporting the usual laundry list of murders, accidents, and political wrongdoings. Every once in a while, they pitched a "feel good" story, and then they noticed their energy perking up when the story aired.

"Why can't we do more inspirational, upbeat news stories?" they asked. Their producer told them to stick to the usual news.

Marc and Bill finally reached a point where they couldn't bear to do one more segment of the news, so they handed in their resignations. They formed a media company, Bolder Media, with the intention of changing the way people received their news. They had no idea where their next paycheck was going to come from; they just knew they wanted to make an impact by producing inspirational "feel good" stories.

> "Happiness is a choice. Learn to follow your heart. Be grateful. Be kind. Be bold. Have fun, have faith, and be fearless. Take the right kind of chances. Chase your dreams, no matter how big or how small. Success isn't measured by the size of your check or by how many people know your name. It's measured by the joy in your heart and the impact you have on others."
> ~ Marc Middleton

I stumbled upon Growing Bolder's website, www.GrowingBolder.com, while writing my first book. I spent hours on the site, immersed in one positive story after another. It was the perfect inspiration for the metamorphosis I was experiencing at the time: Just months after bemoaning the idea of growing old on my forty-fourth birthday, I experienced a turn-around moment when I unwrapped my long-buried passion and got back into the sport of barefoot water skiing. The stories I read at Growing Bolder simply reinforced my newfound excitement at the idea of growing bolder instead of older. I was now looking forward to the future, instead of thinking it was all going to be a downhill ride.

When I met up with Bill in Florida, his media team filmed my story for a Growing Bolder segment that was shown on over 200 PBS stations and RLTV.

I've been really fortunate to benefit from some great advice and encouragement from Bill whenever we talk. During a recent conversation, I told Bill how I was in a state of flux at the moment, pondering my next direction. Bill casually tossed out some wisdom that I think answers some deep questions of how to find your passion, your life direction, and your purpose.

Bill said:

> We're all sitting around the same table. We all get dealt a hand of cards. Some of us will take those cards and turn them into a winning hand. Some will fold and walk away. Some will throw out some, and focus on the others. Look at your hand. What's in it? What do you have that nobody else does? What are your strengths? Then think, "Who would this help?" Then start out on a path, one step at a time, reassessing all the way, constantly reading those cards and walking in as straight a line as possible....

So take a look at the cards you're holding. What's in your hand? Only you can decide how to play it.

Deb Ingino: Taking Off in a New Direction

Deb Ingino loved her job. For seventeen years as the vice president of a global brand, she traveled the world, training business leaders and seeing the company grow from 50 million to over 500 million. She had come a long way from growing up in the Bronx with six siblings in a two-bedroom apartment.

The success was awesome, but the passion was gone. Here she was at the midlife point, and Deb no longer had the same tug in her heart that pulled her along over the years.

When Deb's fiftieth birthday approached, her husband asked what she wanted for a gift. Deb wasn't looking for tangible items; what she wanted was to make an impact. "Have the guests do a random act of kindness before the party," Deb told her husband.

Later during the party, as she sat in the backyard, listening to her friends and family take turns telling their random acts of kindness stories, Deb realized that by having an impact on others, she had received a gift as well. "Midlife is a great time to reflect on ourselves and how to contribute to the world in the next season of our lives."

The classic "midlife crisis" feeling came over her. Instead of buying a sports car or getting a new hairstyle, Deb started reading and exploring options for starting her own business when she saw life coach Dan Miller on a talk show. She heard Dan talk about his books, *48 Days to the Work You Love* and *No More Dreaded Mondays*.

"I bought his books, listened to his podcasts, and hired him as a coach," Deb said. "We had three coaching sessions, and I was off and racing."

Deb gained clarity quickly. She began to redesign her career path. She knew she loved helping people figure out their strengths and use those strengths to enjoy their careers. It was a coaching skill she had used in her corporate job that most people had enjoyed benefitting from.

Deb started to test the water by taking on coaching clients before and after her working hours. Soon, not only were her clients getting results, but Deb found herself energized with each session.

"I think my gut knew right away that I planned to leave my job. Maybe I could do both for a short time, but I was not likely to do both well for a long time. As soon as I started to feel restless, I knew I was going to leave."

Energy is something Deb believes we need to pay attention to, not only during the transition moments of our lives but when our energy changes.

"Sometimes energy can change from year to year," Deb said. "Dan Miller, every year he takes the bottom 15 percent of what he enjoys the least, gets rid of it, and replaces it with new projects. I think that's something we all need to do on a routine basis."

One of the lessons Deb learned by diving into her passions is that we must continually step outside of that proverbial comfort zone. She explains:

> We often believe our destiny is one path, but I believe anything important takes monumental effort. If you're in a comfort zone, you're probably not doing anything worthwhile. We are capable of doing more than we can even imagine.

> We can change the mindset from "I don't think I can" to "How can I do it, how can I make this work?" That's a huge lesson I had to learn, especially coming from a corporate background used to predictability. Learn new strategies, and new ideas.

In her work as a coach, Deb discovered that most people have the talent and the information they need to accomplish their goals, but what stops them is a lack of confidence, validation, and action. "The strategy itself doesn't bring success; it's the action piece that most people stumble on."

Deb's formula for success is simple: Identify your real strengths, minimize what you don't do well, maximize what you do best, find the real area of your gifts—and you'll get the best results.

Today, Deb is a founding partner with Leadership expert John C. Maxwell and is doing what she loves—coaching and speaking—with leaders and their teams, helping them to leverage their strengths and turn them into results.

It's a long way from that two-bedroom apartment in the Bronx, and she regularly enjoys seeing people transform their lives.

CHAPTER 17

Manifesting Your Passion

> *"Our subconscious minds have no sense of humor, play no jokes and cannot tell the difference between reality and an imagined thought or image. What we continually think about eventually will manifest in our lives."*
>
> ~ Robert Collier

I f you've seen the movie *The Secret*, you're probably familiar with the concept of manifestation. Even though I saw the movie when it first was released, I don't think I paid attention to that word until I took

Debra Poneman's "Yes to Success" workshop. Looking back on the list, I realized many of the things had indeed manifested—especially those I put my attention on. Where attention goes, energy flows.

Take Dean Kamen, the inventor of the Segway. He had big dreams when he was a child. He dreamed of a house with secret staircases and a helicopter parked inside. To his teachers, he seemed to be a struggling student and his grades were not stellar. Dean spent his days doing what he could do best: inventing new products. Today, his current house has big glass walls, secret staircases, and a helicopter parked inside. From an early age, he manifested his future. Sure enough, as an adult, he was living his dream life.

Here's what I'm learning every day: you must see the vision in your mind before it can manifest in reality.

Shaun Proulx: Manifesting an Interview with Oprah

I crossed paths with Shaun Proulx on Facebook after seeing a post about his upcoming interview with Oprah on his weekly SiriusXM talk show, *The Shaun Proulx Show*.

Who is this guy, and how in the world did he end up interviewing the elusive Oprah? I wondered. As far as I knew, Oprah didn't give interviews to just anybody.

From what I could see on his Facebook page, Shaun looked like one happy guy who was living a passionate life.

I reached out to Shaun and learned his story:

"I was not always happy—happiness is my success barometer," Shaun began. "When I wake up excited for the day, the month, the year—that, for me, is success."

Before he was even thirty, Shaun was living a luxurious life, working in finance and making lots of money. Even though he had flunked tenth grade math, Shaun had a job dealing with numbers every day. "I owned a house, had a wallet full of credit cards, I traveled all the time—I had everything," Shaun said. He had come a long way from his early struggles of being bullied at school and then coming home to an alcoholic father who berated him.

But despite his high salary and material rewards, deep inside, something was missing for Shaun. He was completely out of alignment with his work and his life. He knew he wasn't meant to be in the world of finance. The job represented a safe life. He felt no passion for his work.

"If you aren't seeing the world through passionate eyes, you are out of alignment," Shaun explained. "To the degree that you feel negative emotions, that is the degree you are out of alignment."

Shaun looked back in his past to find the clues he needed to create a life in a new direction. For ten years, he had put aside his creative skills to chase the almighty dollar. "The mark of a rich man is not how much money he has; it is how much happiness he has," Shaun told me.

Shaun found a clue in his past: He loved acting. The more he contemplated his life path, the more he realized he was meant to be a communicator. He signed up for acting classes, and the minute he walked into the studio for the first class, he was at home. "The very second I stepped into that room, I knew there was no turning back. Even though I didn't quit my job at that instant—I did a few months later—I was hook, line, and sinker into passion at that moment."

Years ago, Shaun was watching *The Oprah Winfrey Show* when Oprah said something profound:

"When you take one step toward the universe, the universe takes nine toward you."

Shaun grabbed a sketch pad and outlined his dreams on paper. He doodled. He wrote. He poured out his heart on paper.

Walking away from the salary and perks of a steady job was scary. Shaun likened it to climbing a cliff and stepping off the edge.

"Passion—that fire-in-the-belly," Shaun told me, "is a feeling that tells you you are on the right track with all that you are and all that you're supposed to be. Passion is your GPS; it tells you that you're in the right place doing the right thing. The Universe/God will tell you 'This is what I want to be; this is what I want to do.' You're ingenious when operating in your passion."

The path became clear for Shaun. A few months later, he walked away from his job and sold his home. He wanted to do meaningful work with passion—work that made his heart sing. His journey led him to create on radio *The Shaun Proulx Show*.

"Butterflies and angels don't grab you and fly you to heaven—you'll have to take the step and you may fall," Shaun said. "But when you're passionate, you'll climb to that edge and it's fun.

"When it comes to manifesting the life you really want, you have to learn to own it," Shaun told me.

"I want everyone to know you can receive things in this world without spending money. Money, in our world, buys you freedom. Money is a man-made concept, and it has no value except the value we assign to it." Shaun gave me an example of how our thoughts manifest into reality: On one of his daily walks, he passed by a neighbor's house and admired her beautiful wreath hanging on the door. He wanted to hire her to make one. The very next day, a new wreath went up on the door. His neighbor was standing by. "I want you to have this," she said. The very thing Shaun admired and desired is now hanging on his door.

"Who makes the sun rise, who makes the planet spin, who makes the tide flow—that's the power you harness when you tap into your passion. Sometimes we separate ourselves from who we really are. When you are passionate about your life, when you are being true to yourself, the world wants you to have what you want."

Using this concept, Shaun set his intention to manifest Oprah into his life. A mutual friend connected them and Shaun invited her on the show. In a full circle moment, Oprah and Shaun talked about the very thing that brought them together: the ability to manifest and align with your dreams.

In the interview, Oprah shared her thoughts on how to align with your passions despite difficult times:

> The very cycle of being a human being means that there are times that you will have clouds; otherwise, you just get blanched or scorched by the sun all the time, and the nature of being human means that there are difficult times. It's like riding the wave, and sometimes it's really smooth, and the ocean is placid, and the waves are great, and everything is wonderful, and sometimes you get knocked off. The real wonderful thing is to know, "Oh, I can find my board and get back on." You know when you are operating in the flow—because the board is your flow.

If You Don't Ask, the Answer Is Always "No"

So you, dear reader, may be wondering how Shaun ended up in this book. That story is a great example of alignment and flow. Shaun showed up in a sponsored ad in my Facebook feed. He was advertising his show with Oprah. Well, I love Oprah. I was able to attend four of her shows in Chicago and had the opportunity to connect with her briefly after the show and thank her for providing sign language interpreters. I've had the opportunity to be published in *O, The Oprah Magazine* three times.

So, as I said earlier, my first thought was, "Who the heck is this Shaun guy and how in the world is he interviewing Oprah?" Oprah doesn't grant very many interviews, but here she was on some Canadian guy's show....

So I set out to read everything I could about Shaun during my lunch break one day. I love people who open their souls with their writing and show the world their gifts. There was something about Shaun that moved me, and I enjoyed his #ThoughtRevolutions, so I sent him an email.

To my surprise, he wrote back and was so friendly that I could feel his warmth shining through. Then my intuition kicked in.

"Ask."

Are you kidding? I can't just ask him for an interview; he doesn't know me, and I haven't taken the time to build a relationship with him yet.

"Ask."

That pesky little voice within would not leave me alone. So I asked. And the answer was "Tell me more about this project."

So I shared my story and the reason behind the book—and Shaun said, "Yes."

That's flow. That's alignment. When it's meant to be, it will be.

But you have to ask. Even when you're trembling inside and thinking too small, you have to ask. Because if you don't, the answer is always, always "No." There's no alignment if you never, ever take a step.

CHAPTER 18

Persisting Through Obstacles

"I certainly don't regret my experiences because without them, I couldn't imagine who or where I would be today. Life is an amazing gift to those who have overcome great obstacles—and attitude is everything."
~ Sasha Azevedo

The Secret to Longevity Behind Passion

Psychologist Angela Lee Duckworth studied children and adults in all kinds of challenging situations in an effort to determine who would achieve success despite less-than-optimal conditions.

She discovered a surprising result.

It doesn't matter what you look like, how social you are, what shape you're in, how much talent you have, or how smart you are....

The one thing that determined success in challenging or extreme situations was...grit.

Grit.

We don't hear that word too often.

In her TED Talk, Angela explained more. "Grit is passion and perseverance for very long-term goals. Grit is having stamina. Grit is sticking with your future, day in, day out, not just for the week, not just for the month, but for years, and working really hard to make that future a reality. Grit is living life like it's a marathon, not a sprint."

Among all of the passionate people I've crossed paths with in the last several years, I've noticed this trait among each of them. The ability to persevere and persist despite obstacles is something that can make the difference between a life of mediocrity and a life of joy.

"Grit is that 'extra something' that separates the most successful people from the rest. It's the passion, perseverance, and stamina that we must channel in order to stick with our dreams until they become a reality."
~ Travis Bradberry

The Quest for Balance

"How do I balance it all?" is a question I'm frequently asked when people first begin to dive into something they're passionate about.

The quest for balance really means, "How can I keep everything going and meet the same needs while doing what I am passionate about?"

You can't. It's physically, emotionally, mentally impossible to do everything, be everything, and feel everything all at once.

And if you're passionately honest about your life, you shouldn't.

Time is a concept that fits into neat little packages. Sixty minutes equals one hour. Twenty-four hours equals one day. And 86,400 seconds also fit into that neat "one day" package. Every second, your life ticks...

Away.

A wise woman once told me to embrace motherhood. "It's a season of your life," she said. Of course, she told me this right smack-dab in the middle of having a baby and two toddlers to deal with.

I just wanted a shower. I just wanted five minutes of peace and quiet to go to the bathroom. I wanted time to think. Time to myself.

"Before you know it, the season will be over and you'll look back on this time and regret that it went by so fast," she said.

And poof!

She was right.

My last child will soon leave the nest. Yes, just like that, my season of "at-home" parenthood is nearly over and moving on to the next.

"There are seasons in life. Don't ever let anyone try to deny you the joy of one season because they believe you should stay in another season.... Listen to yourself. Trust your instincts. Keep your perspective."
~ Jane Clayson

There's a concept called "Leaning In," which embraces the idea that we lean into the curve of where we are going, rather than resisting it and wiping out. Throughout our lives, we will face situations, obstacles, challenges that may not be of our doing. We can choose to lean in and ride through—and choose to see the gifts and blessings that come with the experience.

Sue, one of my closest friends, left two terrible marriages. She was a mom of three kids, two with disabilities. She had no savings since the first divorce wiped her out, but she decided to go back to school and earn a degree in Medical Coding.

During her second divorce, Sue felt like she was drowning—she wanted more from life. Working in a hospital wasn't feeding her soul. Sue sought help from a mentor and went into the insurance business. She faced some great hurdles starting a business from scratch, but today, she feels more alive than ever before.

Sometimes, you have no idea how strong you can be until you stretch yourself. Strength comes from our most trying times...if we have the courage to step into the mess.

Your Obstacles Can Be a Gift to Others

When Rick Hoyt was born, the umbilical cord was twisted around his neck. He spent the first several minutes of his life without oxygen, leaving him unable to speak or walk. The outlook was bleak and his physician suggested putting Rick in an institution for people with disabilities.

Fortunately, Rick's parents were determined to do everything they could to give him access to language.

When Rick was eleven, a team from Tufts University built him a computer that allowed him to type with his head. "Go Bruins!" were the first words he communicated.

During high school, Rick asked his dad, Dick, to push him in a five-mile run for a Lacrosse player who was paralyzed. Like all the other students, Rick wanted to participate to show support for the injured athlete.

Dick wasn't much of a runner, but he gamely pushed his son in a very heavy wheelchair, and together they crossed the finish line, second to last.

Something amazing happened during the race: Disability disappeared for Rick while they ran. He felt free.

That five-mile race would not be their last race—in fact, it was the first of many races, which would turn into thirty-eight years of passion.

When the two of them decided to tackle their first triathlon, there was another challenge: Dick couldn't swim, and he had not been on a bike since he was a kid. Problem solved: The family simply bought a house on a lake and Dick jumped in the water. At first, he couldn't swim more than fifteen feet, but Dick was not one to give up. He persisted until he could swim confidently—then he put Rick in a raft and practiced some more. He adapted a bike and balanced Rick on the front as he pedaled.

Now, most of us can't even fathom doing a triathlon, much less an Ironman. You have to be disciplined, determined, and tough to swim 2.4 miles, bike 112 miles, and then run a 26.2 mile marathon. All without a break—and you must complete the race within seventeen hours.

So I want you to imagine being the athlete who has trained like heck for this race and qualified to compete. Three-fourths of the way through, you've hit a wall. You can't push the bike pedals one more time.

Imagine turning your head to watch Dick pedaling by. He's pushing those pedals with Rick perched on the front of the bike.

One hundred and twenty-five pounds.

That's how much extra weight Dick is teaming up with.

A lightbulb goes off in your head. "If this guy can do it with his son, surely I can find the strength and the energy to do this too."

That's the gift. One person's life path can be a gift to another.

"Passion is love between people," Dick explained. "I have so much passion for my son, there's nothing I wouldn't do for him to help him or to be with him. Rick inspires me and motivates me. The easiest thing for him is to give up, but he's a fighter. That's how it should be. He's included; that's how it should be. We live and play just like everyone else. We've impacted people around the world—and that's a passion for us."

There's no telling how widespread Team Hoyt's impact has been over the many years. Dick and Rick have completed over 1,000 races, including 255 triathlons, 72 Boston Marathons, and 6 Ironmans. To top it all off, they ran and biked across America, completing 3,735 miles in forty-five days.

During our interview, I asked Dick whether he had ever held back in fear when facing something new or unknown. "Was there any doubt that you would finish when you faced your first Ironman?" I asked.

"There was no doubt we would finish," Dick replied. "We prepared physically and mentally. It's especially important to prepare mentally. There's no holding back or fear—we decide what we want to do and go do it. Our message is 'Yes you can.' There's nothing you can't do. There's no word, 'no.'"

Today, back injuries challenge Dick on a daily basis, so he has scaled back on triathlons and long-distances, but he plans to continue to compete with Rick in shorter races as long as he is able.

As for Rick, at age fifty-four, he continues to look forward to upcoming races. "One of the main accomplishments that I would like to do again is complete the Ironman in Kona with my new runner and friend, Bryan Lyons," Rick said.

Throughout their journey, Dick and Rick have been fueled by passion and purpose. "This is the one, single thing that Rick and I were meant to have together," Dick said.

Our journeys matter. Our stories matter. We may not see the gift of our obstacles or challenges, but if we choose to turn them into blessings, some pretty spectacular results will occur.

"Passion is the best answer to pain."
~ **Mike Murdock,** *Secrets of the Richest Man in the World*

CHAPTER 19

When Passion Wanes

"If you have the courage to begin,
you have the courage to succeed."
~ David Viscott

When was the last time you had a spark?

When was the last time you had a change and it was wonderful for you?

Those are the questions life coach Kathy Larson uses when exploring a client's desire for a life of joy and meaning. Kathy trained with Brené Brown, and she is a certified Daring Way Facilitator.

"Most people are looking for their next thing," says Kathy. "They've had some awakening, a breakthrough. They get to a point where they say, 'Enough of this crap! This isn't working. I need help!' They realize they need something different. That's the starting point."

It comes down to what you value, Kathy explained. What do you value? What are you about? How do others describe you—does that fit with what you know to be true about yourself? Dig deep enough into your values and you'll find your passion.

"Passion is a deep sense, almost like a longing. It's something that's really, really hard to control—it's strong—almost like a yearning, a strong feeling that pulls you. It will grab your attention. When you find and define your passion, you can't ignore it. It's a love for something so strong you can't let go of it."

"I believe we are born curious," Kathy explained. "We are born seekers. We are figuring out how to be alive—and our purpose is to learn and discover from that curiosity. When you are clear about your purpose, you can move ahead to fulfilling your purpose with passion. Your passion creates connections in the world."

"But," I asked Kathy, "what happens when passion wanes? What happens when we lose that spark—how do we get it back?"

"With passion," Kathy replied, "many people find it during a crisis. 'Fight or Flight' is turned on. When there's a crisis, that's where we will stand in our strength. And there are times during our life when we step into our purpose, fulfill it, and move on."

The Seasons of Passion

"Passion has a season," David Frey told me in an interview. "As you become older, your passion comes up for different things."

David is known as a marketing guru for small businesses. Our paths crossed through SendOutCards, and I was intrigued by his story because one of his goals was to build a school in Kenya and he made it happen. I could see his passion for life in all of his positive posts on Facebook.

When it comes to passion, the first word that comes to mind is love, meaning you love to do something. David told me, "Passion is love with intensity—when you're passionate about something, you do so with intensity. Passion is something that is self-motivated—it's not someone else nor external circumstances motivating me."

Looking back on his life, David remembers an intense love for basketball. Nothing could keep him away from the court—appointments, rain, a busy schedule—nothing. "I always found time to play basketball because I loved it so much," David said. "If I didn't have time, I would always find the time."

Today, David's passion is directed at family, his spiritual and religious life, and weightlifting. "I read the scriptures and I write my thoughts about that sometimes for two hours every day. When I go to the gym, I typically spend two-and-a-half hours there. Some people say that's too long, that's too much, or that I'm going overboard, but I'm passionate about all of that."

To everything, there is a season, and when it comes to something you're passionate about—that too, can change. Throughout the year, I will sit down with the Passion Test and go through the test to make sure I'm keeping my top five passions current in my life.

Indeed, when passion wanes, it's up to us to determine whether it's a season in our life that we have to close a chapter on, or one that we simply have to take a break from. Remember, feelings ebb and flow. When your energy is low and your drive is gone, that is a time for re-evaluating, re-shifting, and re-focusing. To begin that process, here are two questions to explore:

What's working in your life right now?

_____

_____

What do you want to change?

_____

_____

_____

_____

_____

"In my jobs, I knew it was time to move on when my soul began nudging me in a different direction."
~ Nataly Kogan, Happier, Inc.

One of the biggest myths about passion is that one stays on an ultimate high as a result of living a passionate life. You can't contain a feeling of excitement 24/7. We often associate excitement with passion, yet passion goes deeper. Passion is the sense that says, "This is what I want to do. This is what I'm called to do. This is what I *get* to do." While it's true that, overall, a passionate life is a joyful one, the hard reality is this: We are all on the same roller-coaster we call life.

So what do you do when passion wanes? What do you do when you search deep into your soul and come up with...nothing?

Most likely, that's an indication that something needs to change.

But first...

The Surprising Antidote When Passion Wanes

There's a very simple activity that you can immediately put into practice to bring on an energy shift in your life.

It's a practice that often goes by the wayside; it often takes a backseat in the process of just "getting through the day."

It's the practice of...

Gratitude.

Now, I realize that many self-help books preach this practice. This is likely not the first time you've heard this. But don't be the one who says, "Yeah, yeah," and then go on doing the same old, same old.

This practice works.

When I was at a Tony Robbins seminar, he said something profound: "The antidote to fear is gratitude. The antidote to anger is gratitude. You can't feel fear or anger while feeling gratitude at the same time."

And when passion disappears or wanes, the antidote is gratitude.

Why is that?

Because you can't possibly be grateful without feeling something inside of you. And when you are grateful, the energy shifts. The more gratitude you build up in the daily journey of life, the more momentum you create with the energy inside of you. Sooner or later, you begin to see everything you do, feel, and have—you see everything with appreciation.

The Practice of Gratitude

So what are some ways you can incorporate the practice of gratitude into your life? Over the years, I've added gratitude rituals in different ways. Here, I'll share ten ways you can infuse gratitude into your daily life:

1. **Keep a Gratitude Journal:** Buy a blank, lined journal or a notebook. Leave this on a table next to your bed. Every morning and every evening, write down 3 to 5 things you are grateful for.

2. **Thank You Challenge:** Select a number of people each day and challenge yourself to express verbally your gratitude throughout your day.

3. **Send a Card:** Every single day, send a card to someone. (Of course, I'm partial to SendOutCards. As a gift to you, you can download the app at www.cardsanywhere.com and send a card using this ID code: 125500.)

4. **Stoplights:** At every stoplight, reflect with gratitude on all the good things in your life. (Yes, *every* stoplight!)

5. **The Obscure Thank You:** Do you have a favorite barista at the coffee shop you frequent? What about your chiropractor? How about the secretary at your child's school? Do you know someone who always volunteers their time? Do something to thank that person.

6. **The Gratitude Jar:** Find a large jar and 3 x 5 index cards. Every evening, reflect on something wonderful that happened during the day and give thanks. Write it down and put it in the jar. At the end of the year, open the jar and look back and recognize all the things you've been grateful for during the year.

7. **The Thank You List:** Put on some music or go to a serene place. List 100 things you are immediately grateful for.

8. **The Give-Away:** Give away something that you absolutely love. As hard as it is, you'll be flooded with a grateful feeling that you've never experienced before.

9. **Say Thank You to the Negative:** This one can be tough— but find the gift in the negative experiences and turn it into a positive. For example, the Negative Nellie in your family—say thank you. (No, you don't have to say it out loud.) "Thank

you, Negative Nellie, for you have shown me ways to be the opposite...."

10. **Gratitude for the Now:** The only moment we truly have is the present one. With every breath you take in, breathe gratitude. With every breath you exhale, breathe gratitude.

Start a ReLaunch

During an interview on *The ReLaunch Show* with Joel Boggess and Pei Kang (you'll recall their story in Chapter 3), I asked Jack Canfield to share his most challenging season of life. In my eyes, Jack was a guy who had it made. He partnered with Mark Victor Hansen to create a mega-empire around the Chicken Soup for the Soul books. He authored *The Success Principles,* and he recently released a revised and updated edition of the bestselling book. He was a guy who was surely coasting through life on one success after another.

As it turned out, going through a divorce was Jack's most painful time in life. In an excerpt from *The ReLaunch Show,* Jack shares the story:

> She got all the money; I got to keep my job. So, I was kind of angry, and a little bit bitter, and I teach love and forgiveness and all of that, so it took me probably about, I don't know, three to six months to move through that and get over it, and forgive her and forgive the lawyers, and get to the place where I was at peace with it. But I was wearing shirts, two and three days in a row; I was eating a lot less expensive food than I ever did before; I was really on almost a starvation diet there. But what came out of that, it was really good; it forced me to re-brand myself because we were getting to the place where I wanted to sell Chicken Soup for the Soul; it just wasn't.... The stories weren't inspiring me anymore; it had lost its juice, and that's

when I created The Success Principles and re-branded myself as a Success Coach. And that changed my life in a very positive way, 'cause I knew I had to find some way to rebuild the wealth that I had before I got divorced, and I've been able to do that through this. So, even though it was painful, and I was upset a lot in the beginning, I think it was one of the best things that ever happened to me.

In the process of revising the new edition of *The Success Principles*, Jack discovered he had forgotten some of the very success principles he had written ten years earlier.

> *"Our passions are the true phoenixes;*
> *when the old one is burnt out, a new one*
> *rises from its ashes."*
> ~ Johann Wolfgang von Goethe

Joel and Pei, the hosts of *The ReLaunch Show*, have experienced several passion-centered relaunches in their own lives. Pei enjoyed her career as a dentist, but after many years, she felt restless. There was a strong yearning for more, but she had no idea what "more" was. Pei figured she simply needed a hobby—something to do outside of work. She took up dancing, taught yoga, and volunteered at a therapy dog program.

"At the time, I had a very successful dentistry practice—I had great managers and an assistant, but every day I would go to work and feel like I was in a box—the same old box," Pei said. "I felt my work didn't allow me to use my gifts."

A sweet, Southern lady, who was one of Pei's patients, gave Pei her "awakening moment" by telling her she had truly met her calling—yet Pei felt empty inside. "At that very moment, I was aware that dentistry was not my passion," Pei said.

It took another two years for Pei to explore her soul. She knew she wanted to sell her practice and join Joel in the ReLaunch business, but she kept waiting for the right time and the perfect conditions. Deep into a chapter of Marianne Williamson's *A Return to Love*, Pei found her inspiration for action. "I had been complaining and making excuses all along," Pei said. "I was waiting for something else to happen—giving myself conditions and excuses—I wouldn't change unless something else happened first."

The moment Pei sold her practice, she was filled with a mixture of emotions. On one hand, she felt a sense of liberation and excitement. On the other hand, she faced the scary feeling of the complete unknown ahead.

Today, Joel and Pei have one of the most popular podcasts on the web, and they have won several awards. They both take great satisfaction in helping others to ReLaunch their lives.

"We go through seasons in life, and a passion may only be around for one season," Joel said. "Do yourself, your community, and your family a favor—really take the time to explore the depths of your passion because that is who you are. You are given a passion for a purpose, a reason, and when you discover what that is, everybody benefits—because you are able to get that clarity on what you are about—and then you are able to add value to yourself and to those around you."

"Nothing great in the world has been accomplished without passion."
~ George Hegel

Finding Your Passion Again—and Again

Olympic swimmer Dara Torres unwrapped her passion for swimming at a very young age. As a child, she was drawn to water and started swimming at seven. Sports were always easy for Dara; she was very athletic and highly competitive, but swimming was something special. Swimming captured her heart, and passion fueled every stroke.

"People ask me all the time, 'Where do you get that passion?'" says Dara. "It's not something you learn, it's just there. It's something that's inside of you."

Passion is what drove Dara to set high goals from a very young age—she wanted to set new records and compete in the Olympics. At fourteen, she set a national record, and by seventeen, she was competing in the Olympics.

During her swimming career, Dara hung up her suit twice, missing the 1996 and 2004 Olympics. When she returned to the Olympics at thirty-three, she discovered it was much more difficult to train at the same level as the younger swimmers, so she learned to swim smarter instead. At the age of forty, Dara decided to make another comeback and aim for the Olympics once again, but this time, she had a baby in her life and had endured shoulder and knee surgeries. Her teammates jokingly called her "Grandma."

Just three weeks after giving birth, Dara swam in a meet. Fifteen months later, Dara broke her own record, the one she set back as a teen. Over her career, she racked up twelve Olympic medals.

Passion is what kept Dara driven throughout her swimming career, but there were times when her excitement and desire disappeared completely. She no longer wanted to do laps. Every lap felt agonizingly long. Her heart just wasn't in it anymore. When she had reached that point three times in her career, she knew it was time to step back and hang up the suit. What she discovered is that a break was just what she needed to fire up the desire again.

I asked Dara whether every competitive swimmer or Olympian has passion.

"No," she said. "Some swimmers get into the sport because of parents and only continue to the next level because of a scholarship or other external factors. It's easy to see who has passion and who doesn't—you can see it with everything they do. As I get older," Dara added, "I notice it more."

At forty-five, Dara tried out for the Olympics for the sixth time, but she missed the team by just .09 of a second.

Today, Dara has immersed herself in a new passion, joining the first all-female sports talk show on CBS, *We Need to Talk*. At first, she found herself completely out of her comfort zone and challenged to step up her game with each episode on the air. "It's okay to feel that intimidation—it's a different feeling to experience," Dara said. "It's a 'growing' feeling—it makes me grow as a person."

As she moves away from the structured life of her swimming career, Dara continues to explore new options and activities.

"It's nice to take a winding path and see where life takes you—and not have a plan all the time; that's a good thing."

The Passion Rut

So what can you do if you find yourself in a Passion Rut?

A couple of years after putting my feet back on the water, I found myself dreading my next competition. Every time I got into the water to train, I was cranky. My skiing partners noticed it. "Relax! This is supposed to be fun," they reminded me.

I wasn't having fun. I was miserable. I didn't even know why I was competing anymore—because I no longer had the hunger to improve. The thought of driving five hours and staying three days to compete in four fifteen-second runs simply drained me of energy.

Had I lost my passion for the sport?

When passion wanes, there are three things you can do:

1. **Take a break:** Hit the "pause" button or completely back off. Sometimes a break is all that is needed to create a void or restart the flame.
2. **Do a reality check:** If you completely quit or walked away, where would you be without this passion in your life? What regret would result?
3. **Reinvent or shift direction:** Change the way you experience passion in your life. Shift in a new direction or add something new to the journey. Do a pivot and explore a whole new path with your passion.

In my case, I took a break at first. I stopped competing, yet I still stayed involved by being on a committee that selected competitors for awards and I managed a Facebook site for barefooting.

After a while, I realized I needed a challenge. I wanted to do something fun with the sport, and something that would stretch me. I wanted something that I could accomplish and something to strive for.

I came up with a quest: I would barefoot water ski in all fifty states during my fiftieth decade.

The minute I came up with that quest, all the passion came flooding back. I would be able to travel, to meet new people, and to barefoot water ski in many different places! I had no clue HOW I would accomplish the quest; I simply focused on the WHAT. Sure enough, people began inviting me to their states and offering to pull me. As of this writing, I've barefoot water skied in twelve states. It's been a lot of passionate fun!

CHAPTER 20

Rippling Your Passion

> "Each choice we make causes a
> ripple effect in our lives. When things
> happen to us, it is the reaction we
> choose that can create the difference
> between the sorrows of our past and
> the joy in our future."
> ~ Chelle Thompson

Passion is energy. You invite that energy into your life by conscious choice. A rock dropped into a glassy, calm pond creates an implosion of energy that pops back on to the surface and spreads outward. First one ripple, then another, and another.

Andy Andrews has a book about this: *The Butterfly Effect*. One simple flap of a butterfly's wings can create a ripple that is felt on the other side of the world. A person who uses his gift of passion has a positive effect that generates a ripple that goes on and on.

I'm a firm believer that passion is entwined with purpose. And purpose gives life meaning. Sometimes it takes a lifetime to understand our purpose, but we certainly don't have to wait to experience passion and joy. At any given moment, we have the power to change our thoughts, our attitudes, or our actions to create the journey we want.

Let me tell you about Ann O'Brine Satterfield. I met Ann at a water skiing event in Wisconsin. A group of us had gathered for a training on how to work with people with disabilities so they can enjoy the sport of water skiing.

I sat in the front row, feeling quite intimidated as I watched Ann bark out orders with the sharp confidence of a drill sergeant. In a short time, all the adaptive skis were lined up and the ropes laid out with precision. An hour later, we knew all the safety rules and we were ready for the first skier of the day.

Ann is legendary in the sport, both as a competitive tournament skier and the founder of the adaptive water ski program, U Can Ski 2. She has won many awards and been inducted into the Water Ski Hall of Fame.

A bout of polio as a child rendered Ann unable to walk, and she grew up using a wheelchair. In her late thirties, Ann discovered freedom on the water when she learned to water ski using a ski that was adapted for her. She was the first adaptive skier to go over a jump and land it. Ann trained competitively, winning the National Championship five times and the World Championship twice. When she retired from competition, she decided to pay it forward. She wanted to use her passion to help others enjoy freedom on the water, too.

For over twenty-five years, Ann did just that. She trained hundreds of side-skiers to ski alongside thousands of people with disabilities.

One day, Ann asked me to help her work with a deaf woman who wanted to learn to water ski again. We spent an afternoon on the water together. Ann drove and I worked as a side skier. On the last run, the woman skied by herself. She had the biggest smile on her face. Ann sported an even bigger smile. We went around and around the lake—seven times. In the middle of it all, I captured a picture of Ann. She had passion written all over her face. She was blissfully content because she was doing something she truly loved to do.

During a recent trip down to Florida, I stopped in to see Ann. She was wrapping up the last adaptive ski clinic of the year and looking forward to the holidays with her family before starting up another round of clinics in the new year.

A few weeks later, out of the blue, a mutual friend contacted me to let me know some shocking news: Ann was in the last days of her life. She had been diagnosed with cancer a year and half before and had not shared it publicly. In the previous week, doctors discovered the cancer had spread rapidly throughout her body.

On her last boat ride with several friends, Ann reminisced about her life and her work. She had touched so many lives, both on the water and off.

"I was blessed," Ann told my friend. "Because I went from 'Why me, in the wheelchair?' to 'Oh, this is why; *this* is my mission.'"

What's *Your* Mission?

What about you? What's your mission?

The whole "Mission Statement" stuff used to trip me up whenever I attempted to write one out. I often felt like I had too many missions rolled into one sentence.

One day, during a board and staff meeting for a non-profit organization that I work for, we spent a lot of time going back and forth crafting a mission statement.

Then in a moment of clarity, I realized what it really was about: When we strip everything away and get down to the nitty gritty—what are we about? At that very moment, the mission for that organization became crystal clear. We just have to take away the fancy words and arrive at the purpose.

As for me, I'm all about passion. I'm all about helping others to unwrap their passions and create the life they truly want to live.

Now, what about you? What are you about?

_____

_____

_____

_____

_____

_____

Drew Dudley: Lollipop Moments

When Drew Dudley was in college, he started planning events and leading fundraisers—and he discovered he had a talent for it. Because of his natural talent for gathering a group of people to work together for a common cause, he figured he should select that route as a career.

Then someone asked him to do a speech about leadership.

"I thought to myself, 'I'm not really a leader,'" Drew said. "I called up a friend for advice because I didn't know what to say."

His friend gave him a suggestion: Talk about *not* being a leader.

But the more Drew thought about it, the more he realized that yes, he was a leader, but he had simply been defining the word too narrowly. Instead of thinking of a leader as someone who impacts large crowds of people and does work that changes the entire world, a leader can actually have an impact on just one person.

"All too often, we define leaders on a very narrow basis, so many people overlook the title of leader, even when they are actually leading others," Drew explained.

His work on leadership led to a TED Talk called "Leading with Lollipops."

During a college registration day, Drew was handing out lollipops to the students waiting in line. One freshman student was ready to head back home, convinced that college life was not for her. Drew handed a lollipop to a male student standing next to her and said, "You need to give a lollipop to the beautiful woman standing next to you."

As soon as the lollipop was in the girl's hand, Drew turned to her parents and quipped, "Look at that. Look at that. First day away from home and already she's taking candy from a stranger!"

Laughter erupted. The girl dated the guy from that moment on. Four years later, she contacted Drew to thank him for that lollipop moment.

Drew didn't remember any of it. It was just a moment of being himself, of making someone laugh, of making the process easier for new students.

But it changed her life. Drew was invited to their wedding a year-and-a-half later.

As Drew said in his TED Talk:

How many of you guys have a lollipop moment? A moment where someone said something or did something that you feel fundamentally made your life better?

We need to redefine leadership as being about lollipop moments, how many of them we create, how many of them we acknowledge, how many of them we pay forward, and how many of them we say thank you for. Because we've made leadership about changing the world, and there is no world; there are only six billion understandings of it. And if you change one person's understanding of it, one person's understanding of what they're capable of, one person's understanding of how much people care about them, one person's understanding of how powerful an agent of change they can be in this world, you've changed the whole thing.

Think about it. Every single day, we are being mentored and led in more ways than we know, and sometimes, we aren't even aware of it. A kind word from someone. Encouragement from a coach. An inspirational passage from a book you read. (Hey, it could be this one.)

After watching Drew's TED Talk, my intuition kicked in and I reached out to talk to him. I was fortunate to catch him on a sabbatical in Savannah, Georgia. So, naturally, we talked about passion and what it means. Here's what Drew shared:

> When you do something that brings in more energy than it takes away, that's passion. Even if you're exhausted, passion can generate energy for you instead of taking it away.

> I can think of occasions when I wasn't really excited to do what I do. I was either exhausted or sick or at the end of a long trip. Once I started speaking, the exhaustion went away. Passion means having your own internal generator—it doesn't matter if you're tired—when you start something you're passionate about, you're energized.

I'm passionate about encouraging people to know their own stories. I'm passionate about long walks in the afternoon—that's a new one for me—I get more energy at the end of the walk. I like long trips on back roads, listening to music, and meditation.

Sometimes I ask myself that question—what's my dream? I'm living that dream. I also create new dreams. Don't worry about five-year plans—focus on five-year momentum. You always have to keep momentum and continually move forward.

What worries me is that people talk about passion like it's a magical thing. "Follow your passion" is terrible career advice if you have no idea what you're passionate about. You often become passionate when you're doing things that are important to you. Passion takes hard work, and the thing you're passionate about often shows up after you work hard to become good enough. You can't just wander around hoping you'll find it—you have to keep trying new things and sometimes fail—and then finally discover it. You have to take action. You can't just "hope" you find your passion.

And passion is not just one single thing. You can have many different passions in your life—you have a huge ability for passion—passion is innate. We can be filled by many things. Passion means to generate energy. Fill your life with as many passions as possible.

If you haven't yet found one thing you're passionate about, our failure is if we don't keep seeking it. Patience. You may think "My life isn't complete," but passion will come up many times in your life. Just because you've found one passion doesn't mean you've accomplished your mission.

I can't picture the rest of my life without my speaking career, but eleven years ago, I couldn't even picture myself speaking, and now it's important to me. I have found a life of passion, but I don't say that I've found *the* passion.

You should not search for one great passion—but passion must always be a part of your life. It will take on many different forms. Finding your passion can lead to new passions too—it can lead to new things in your life. There's not just one place to call home, not just one person to love—we have the amazing capacity to keep looking and experiencing passion in different ways.

Activity:
Which activities generate energy in your life?

_____

_____

_____

_____

_____

_____

_____

Steve Harper: Creating the Ripple Effect

When Steve Harper was in high school, he dreamed of becoming a professional soccer player, but a blow to his knee dashed his future on the field. While Steve was in high school, his father gave him a book, *Swim with the Sharks Without Being Eaten Alive*. Right then and there,

Steve developed a passion for business. He became an entrepreneur at twenty-two and hasn't looked back.

After selling two of his companies, Steve wanted to create a company with a meaningful impact. He formed Ripple Central, a company that teaches others to build and foster connections in innovative ways. "I wanted to share the concept of the ripple effect—of people creating value within relationships and networks, appreciating that everyone you come across in life and business has the power to make an impact in your world, and you in theirs," Steve said.

Steve encounters a lot of clients who are seeking career transitions, but they have no idea what to do or simply feel stuck where they are. "I hear people say, 'I don't know what I'm passionate about,' and they struggle because Oprah tells you you're supposed to follow your true calling and they see others follow their bliss and passion—and they feel let down," Steve said. "Many people don't take the time to slow down and actually think about the activities that bring them happiness."

Early in his journey as a speaker, Steve wasn't sure he was making an impact. A few years later, people began coming up to him and telling him, "You changed my life."

One particular speaking gig made an impact seven years later. As Steve prepared to speak, a woman came up to him to compliment him on his speaking growth and improvement.

"You were really good seven years ago," she said, "but I saw a completely different person today. The stories you wove in make the message so powerful."

She began to cry.

"Is something wrong?" Steve asked.

"You don't realize it, but back then, I was going through some hard changes with my career, but you gave me the courage to go out and create relationships with people. I'm doing something now that I'm passionate about. I feel like I'm making a difference. You started that ripple seven years ago, and it continues to ripple today."

And that's exactly what Steve intended when he created his business, The Ripple Effect. What you do matters. You may not immediately see the effect of your words, your actions, or your gifts, but you have the ability to make a difference.

> *"Passion, it's the fire in your belly that starts deep in your soul and connects with your heart. Passion shows the light in your heart and becomes a tangible action in your life."*
> ~ **Steve Harper**

Keeping Passion in Your Life: The UNWRAP Formula

The process of unwrapping your passion is simple. We just *think* it's complicated. We are each born with unlimited gifts—it's up to us to unwrap them. There's no end to discovering what's inside of us, what we're capable of, and what we can dream up.

I want to introduce you to George Blair. I never had the opportunity to meet George, but of all the people I've interviewed, I think George's Passion Meter was off the charts. He was full of passion from the day he was born until he took his last breath at the age of ninety-eight.

George is the guy who invented the idea of taking baby pictures at hospitals. At the age of forty, while recovering from back surgery, he water skied for the first time. Six years later, he ditched the skis and learned to barefoot ski.

George lived with so much passion that his energy overflowed. He was a savvy entrepreneur with a love for everything yellow. A yellow house. A yellow car. A yellow boat. Yellow clothes. Yellow bananas. In fact, he became known as "Banana George." He traveled all over the world, barefooting in forty-five countries. He was the first guy to barefoot water ski on all seven continents.

As George became older, he became even more passionate about learning new things. Snowboarding. Flying a plane solo. Riding a bull. Racing cars. Riding a camel. Skydiving. Surfing.

He broke his back four times. Yes, you read that right, *four* times. He endured eleven broken ribs, a broken knee, and a broken ankle.

Most people probably would have stopped after the first broken back and adjusted to a slowed-down lifestyle.

Nothing stopped George. He barefoot water skied until he was ninety-three. When he could no longer stand on the water, he switched to a sit-ski. His motto was simple: Don't wait for the next thing; *make* the next thing happen!"

Even after George had a stroke, his passion continued to show. Every single day, his wife or his caregiver pushed his wheelchair on the streets of New York City so he could listen to live jazz music. The blog "Humans of New York" featured him in a story. Until he took his last breath at the age of ninety-eight, George Blair lived a very full life.

No matter what your age is, you can choose to live fully. Ignore the candles on your cake and, instead, rejoice in what you *can* do. Choose in favor of your passions.

I developed the UNWRAP formula to help keep you on track to living a passionate life:

U: Understand. Understand what you're passionate about. Be clear about what you want and what brings you joy.

N: Nurture. Nurture yourself. Your dreams are important. You matter.

W: Wonder. Keep the wonder in your life. Begin with a beginner's mind. Curiosity, exploration, and constant learning will keep the journey fresh.

R: Reflect, Re-evaluate, Renew. Reflect on the journey. Re-evaluate. When you're off path, off purpose, adjust the course. Renew and begin again in a new direction.

A: Awe. Invite more awe moments into your life. It puts the *awe* in an *awesome* life.

P: Passion. Live each day with passion. This will guide you and free you with everything you do. Remember Janet Attwood's advice: "Whenever you're faced with a choice, decision, or opportunity, choose in favor of your passions."

A FINAL NOTE

"There is no passion to be found playing small—in settling for a life that is less than the one you are capable of living."
~ Nelson Mandela

Years ago, when I first started my passion journey, I had the idea to write this book. I could clearly see the title: *Unwrapping Your Passion*. The problem was that, at the time, I didn't know very many people living a passionate life. I knew the time wasn't yet right to begin the book. So I wrote nine other books instead.

One day, I reached out to Kevin Hall, the author of *Aspire*, with my dilemma. He told me to dive into the path and that people would appear in my life to help me. If you remember from the first chapter, he shared a Joseph Campbell quote:

"Follow your bliss and the universe will open doors
for you where there were only walls."

Shortly after he said that, the first person I interviewed, Pete Gluszek, showed up on the last seat of the very next flight I took. He left a job as an environmental engineer to become a pro fisherman. Since then, I've had the pleasure of meeting many, many people living passionate lives.

I had the opportunity to meet Kevin for the first time when I attended his Genshai Life Mastery Experience in Utah. The event took place at a beautiful resort deep in a canyon. We spent three days and two nights intensely immersed in the learning process of sharpening our path and our purpose.

One evening, we were treated to a concert by Romayne Wheeler, a pianist, composer, writer, and researcher who is best known for life and work with the Tarahumara people in the Mexican state of Chihuahua.

The high walls of rock amplified the piano notes beautifully. Passion and bliss were etched into Romayne's face as his fingers danced across the keys. The hours and hours and years and years of honing his skill at the piano were evident in the joy and wonder that I saw on people's faces around me. The beautiful music was a gift to everyone there.

That's what happens when you step into your passion. God has made you so beautifully unique that there is no one else just like you. When you deny yourself a passionate life, you withhold your gifts, skills, talents, and abilities from the world.

You may have noticed at the very beginning of this book that it is dedicated to Patti Phadke. Patti and I shared a love of books, so we met up every six weeks with the BookHands book club composed of deaf women in the Chicago area.

During one book club meeting, we discussed the topic of happiness. The book that month was *What Happy Women Know*. One by one, we went around the room discussing our passions and big dreams. What would it take for us to be happy?

"We have to choose to be happy," Patti said.

Happiness is present when you are living with passion and serving your purpose.

Patti's passion was so clear: her passion was being a mom. Patti was a mom of four kids. There was no time to waste since her days were filled with school activities, sports, and homework. Patti believed her purpose and her passion was motherhood, and she loved every aspect of it. She was blissfully happy and content being a mom.

"Okay, so when the kids are grown and on their own, then what will your passion shift to," I persisted. "What's a big thing you want to do, or a dream that you have?"

"Perhaps work on an organic farm in Maine," she said since she liked to garden and grow fruits and vegetables.

A few years later, Patti reached the empty nest stage. Her last kid went off to college, one daughter became engaged, and the family welcomed two new grandchildren from another daughter. Patti took a teaching job at a college. Life was humming along beautifully. One day, Patti went to the dentist and mentioned that she had a sore in her mouth that didn't seem to want to heal.

A biopsy revealed some startling news: stage four cancer. Patti spent a lot of time with her family and extended family as she went through treatment. The treatment seemed to be working as the tumor was shrinking.

Then one morning, she woke up and the tumor had multiplied. There was no stopping it now; it spread with a vengeance. Patti was in tremendous pain at times, but she powered through it, determined to stay strong for her family.

We held our last BookHands meeting at my house and included the spouses. Patti only had days left to live, but that night, she was full of energy. We decided to do something fun and each of us took turns asking silly questions that we all had to answer. For four hours, we laughed and learned new things about each other.

I am so sad that we no longer have her beautiful presence on this earth. I miss her. Patti was an amazing mom. Motherhood was everything to her—she found her joy in small ways and big ways—and she embraced that path with passion. Patti taught me that passion doesn't just have to be the fire in the belly—passion is also the quiet nudging of the heart. We just have to listen.

The impact of a book is always a hit or miss with readers. Some walk away thinking, "I finally finished it." Others yearn for more—they don't want it to end.

I hope you close this final chapter with a satisfied smile and the eager anticipation of passionate days ahead. It would break my heart if you were to close this book and settle back into a ho-hum routine again. As you learned earlier, passion is both a feeling as well as a way of living. Choose in favor of your passions and joy will certainly accompany you on your journey.

The average person goes to his grave with the music still in him, Oliver Wendell Holmes tells us. Share your gifts, talents, skills, and beautiful energy with the world. Go through your life journey with passion and bliss as your companions.

It is my hope that the words in this book have touched you in a way that inspires you. I hope you wake up each day with the intention of living in joy and contentment. I hope you live with passion.

Passion is energy. At any given moment, you can choose to tap into it. Passion is the gift within you—unwrap yours.

ACKNOWLEDGMENTS

No one ever succeeds alone. I was fortunate to cross paths with so many wonderful, passionate people who helped me pave a beautiful journey with this book.

First and foremost is my family—especially my husband. Joe has been by my side since we were teenagers, and he has been the Chief Encouragement Officer for this project. Whenever I expressed frustration, doubt, or discouragement, Joe stepped in and kept me going. This book is for my children: David, Lauren, and Steven—may you continue to live with passion. A special thank you to Lauren, who read the manuscript and advised me on changes.

To Debra Poneman and Janet Attwood, I am humbly grateful for your lessons on passion, for the two of you taught me a whole new way to live.

Thank you, Kevin Hall, for your guidance, wisdom, and mentorship on this journey.

Appreciation and big thanks to Dan Miller, for it was your books and workshop that prompted me to take action on my writing dreams.

To Judy Myers and Keith St. Onge, thank you for re-igniting the spark of passion for my beloved sport of barefoot water skiing. Without you two, this book might have never been written.

Thank you, Jackie St. Onge, for the many phone calls and for giving me the most beautiful definition of passion, part of which became the title of this book.

To Jackie Wellwood (writing buddy) and Tyler Tichelaar (editor), thank you for shaping the progress of this book. Thank you, Matt Odom of Pixel Perfect Pros for bringing my first vision of a cover to life--which inspired the final cover.

A big thank you to Diane Brogan for providing advice and insight when I was near completion. Your daily texts each morning gave me the energy I needed when everything seemed overwhelming.

To the awesome team at Morgan James Publishing, thank you for taking this manuscript from a few hundred words on a Word document to a published book in every format.

To all of the passionate people I've met, interviewed, and connected with, thank you for openly sharing your stories for this book. Your wisdom, advice, and definitions of passion shaped this into a beautiful book.

And to you, dear reader, I thank you for having the courage to explore a topic that can truly evoke a positive change. May you share your passionate energy with the world.

To Introduce and Keep Passion in Your Life

Andrews, Andy. *The Little Things, Why You Should Really Sweat the Small Stuff.*

Attwood, Janet and Chris. *The Passion Test: The Effortless Path to Discovering Your Life Purpose.*

Baker, Dan and Stauth, Cameron. *What Happy People Know: How the New Science of Happiness Can Change Your Life for the Better.*

Boggess, Joel. *Finding Your Voice.*

Brown, Brené. *The Gifts of Imperfection.*

Branson, Richard. *Like a Virgin, Secrets They Won't Teach You at Business School.*

Canfield, Jack. *The Success Principles.*

Dyer, Wayne. *I Can See Clearly Now.*

Fields, Jonathan. *How to Life a Good Life.*

Goins, Jeff. *The Art of Work.*

Gage, Randy. *Why You're Dumb, Sick, and Broke…and How to Get Smart, Healthy, and Rich.*

Hadaway, Terry. *Live Your Why.*

Hall, Kevin. *Aspire: Uncovering Your Purpose Through the Power of Words.*

Hardy, Darren. *The Compound Effect.*

Hawk, Tony. *How Did I Get Here?: The Ascent of an Unlikely CEO.*

Maxwell, John. *The 15 Invaluable Laws of Growth: Live Them and Reach Your Potential.*

Miller, Dan. *48 Days to the Work You Love: Preparing for the New Normal.*

———. *No More Dreaded Mondays: Fire Yourself—and Other Revolutionary Ways to Discover Your True Calling at Work.*

———. *Wisdom Meets Passion.*

Murdock, Mike. *Secrets of the Richest Man in the World.*

Olsher, Steve. *What is Your WHAT?*

Orloff, Judith. *Positive Energy.*

Partridge, Howard. *Seven Secrets of a Phenomenal L.I.F.E.*

Schmiff, Marcia. *Happy for No Reason.*

Slim, Pam. *Body of Work, Finding the Thread that Ties Your Story Together.*

Sincero, Jen. *You Are a Badass, How to Stop Doubting Your Greatness and Live an Awesome Life.*

Tracy, Brian. *Goals: How to Get Everything You Want Faster Than You Thought Possible.*

Wilkerson, Carrie. *The Barefoot Executive.*

Ziglar, Tom and Zig. *Born to Win.*

OTHER BOOKS

by Karen Putz

Gliding Soles (with Keith St. Onge)

The Passionate Lives of Deaf and Hard of Hearing People

The Parenting Journey: Raising Deaf and Hard of Hearing Children

Barefoot Water Skiing: From Weekend Warrior to Competitor

Global Voices of Social Media

The Helen Keller Collection

Living with Passion

In Pursuit of Passion

Getting Paid to Play

ABOUT THE AUTHOR

Karen Putz was born with normal hearing and began losing her hearing in elementary school. She became deaf as a teen after taking a hard fall while barefoot water skiing. At the age of forty-four, she rediscovered her passion for the sport and put her feet back on the water again.

Karen is known as *The Passion Mentor*, and her mission is to help others unwrap their passions and create joyful, happy lives at any age. Karen speaks on this topic internationally.

Karen and her husband are the parents of three children and one adorable Westie.

You can visit Karen at her website:
www.UnwrappingYourPassion.com.

To request Karen for a speaking engagement:
karen@agelesspassions.com

Morgan James
Speakers Group

We connect Morgan James published
authors with live and online events
and audiences whom will benefit
from their expertise.